THE MYTH OF
DEPRESSION AS DISEASE

D0075395

Recent Titles in
Contemporary Psychology

THE MYTH OF DEPRESSION AS DISEASE

Limitations and Alternatives to Drug Treatment

Allan M. Leventhal and Christopher R. Martell

Foreword by Marsha Linehan

Contemporary Psychology
Chris E. Stout, Series Editor

Westport, Connecticut
London

Library of Congress Cataloging-in-Publication Data

Leventhal, Allan M.
   The myth of depression as disease : limitations and alternatives to drug
treatment / Allan M. Leventhal and Christopher R. Martell ; foreword by Marsha
Linehan.
      p. cm. — (Contemporary psychology, ISSN 1546-668X)
   Includes bibliographical references and index.
   ISBN 0-275-98976-3 (hardcover)
   1. Depression, Mental—Treatment—Evaluation. 2. Depression,
Mental—Chemotherapy—Evaluation. 3. Antidepressants—Effectiveness.
4. Cognitive therapy. I. Martell, Christopher R. II. Title. III. Series: Contemporary
psychology (Praeger Publishers)
RC537.L477   2006
362.2′5—dc22   2005025630

British Library Cataloguing in Publication Data is available.

Library of Congress Catalog Card Number: 2005025630
ISBN: 0–275–98976–3
ISSN: 1546–668X

First published in 2006

Praeger Publishers, 88 Post Road West, Westport, CT 06881
An imprint of Greenwood Publishing Group, Inc.
www.praeger.com

Printed in the United States of America

The paper used in this book complies with the
Permanent Paper Standard issued by the National
Information Standards Organization (Z39.48–1984).

10   9   8   7   6   5   4   3   2   1

CONTENTS

SERIES FOREWORD

As Series Editor of Contemporary Psychology for Praeger, I am in the very fortunate position of being able to read a number of fantastic book concepts and manuscripts. Of course, I also read some proposals or manuscripts not quite ready for publication or inappropriate for this series. At first blush, just reading the title, I thought this book was going to be in the latter category. However, reading the text, I came to understand this is not a diatribe providing a Manichaean view of psychology versus biology, or therapy versus pills. This is a book that takes sound shots at some sacrosanct viewpoints and a couple of sacred cows. It is a volume that provides readers with a proverbial informed consent as to differential therapeutics and treatment selection factors. It serves as an informational empowerment tool for consumers to get clear answers for common questions—and thus be in a much better position of choice. This is good.

This is precisely the kind of book that the Contemporary Psychology series looks to publish. We seek to give voice and venue to authoritative work, not by necessity of mainstream or popular thought. And this book fits the bill. It is not a book of indiscriminate possibilism or trite, feel-good nostrums. Its arguments are offered with support and scholarship, not mere opinion.

Soundness aside, we know the arguments will not be popular with opponents.

We all have our biases.

Initially, my personal bias meant I was critical of the pharmaceutical-medical-industrial-complex-conspiracy-theory angle herein. I don't generally agree with tyranny-of-the-majority views. I don't oppose "Big pharma," nor do I doubt that depression is biological or an illness. In the spirit of full disclosure and transparency, I am psychologically trained and adhere to a cognitive-behavioral, ecological-systems approach. I know there is a body of peer-reviewed literature describing how psychotherapy can change brain functioning, if not actual anatomy. I also know psycho-neuroimmunology demonstrates that psychological interventions can go far in impacting biological functioning.

Nevertheless, I see this book's application and execution as critically helpful to those with depression, as well as for graduate students and clinicians.

In some way, it's a bit ironic. In the 1980s I found myself writing articles and op-ed pieces to convince the lay population that depression was real, that psychotherapy was real, and that good diagnostics and managing outcomes is the way to optimize treatment. Back then many thought of psychotherapy as "buying a friendship," or being psychoanalyzed, or some other snake oil poultice for the soul or psyche. Indeed, the decade earlier had nude encounter groups, hot tub therapy, and est for goodness sake. Medications were in a nascent state and "mother's little helpers" ruled in the proverbial Valley of the Dolls. I worked and wrote to beat the drum of legitimacy, science, and reason for psychological interventions. Fast forward to today and perhaps the pendulum is not swinging back but rather in a circle. That is, we have a much more mature and robust scientific clinical literature, better efficacy studies, a consumer empowerment movement, more psycho-pharmacological interventions, and evidence-based practices—but we're still wrapped in controversy and turf-battles, and some psychotherapies are still suspect.

Good information goes a long way to enhance lasting change.

To my way of thinking then, this book can serve as a valuable tool in offering a utilitarian option for those in need.

Chris E. Stout
Series Editor

FOREWORD

The field of mental health research and care has progressed in fits and starts over the last several decades. At its best, when supported by sound research, treatments have improved and have been developed that outperform the standards of care from the past. At its worst, ideas, treatment philosophies, and practice guidelines have become ingrained as truisms that lack empirical support, but are erroneously accepted as based on fact. The belief that we already know how to treat a problem or disorder can become the enemy of finding out how to do it better.

One of the more exciting advances in recent years is the emergence of the neurosciences as a partner with the behavioral sciences in both developing new treatment paradigms and in researching the mechanisms of action among current effective treatments. In considering the wedding of neuroscience with behavioral science and its impact on mental health treatments, a number of factors must be remembered. First, all human action and reaction, including observable behaviors, emotional responses, thoughts, images, and sensations, are biological events. That is, there is nothing human (or animal of any kind) that is not biological. Nor is there any human activity that does not involve some sort of neural firing in the brain. With the advent of the newer and more powerful methodologies of the neurosciences emerging over the last several decades, the intimate relationship of neural firing of the brain with thought, emotion, and action became clear to both the scientific community and the public. The 1990s were called the decade of the brain. The promise was that with these new sciences, we would be able to control our actions, reactions, moods, and perhaps even our ultimate happiness and destiny by controlling our brains. No doubt it is true: if one can find a way to exert control over one's own brain, one could control much if not all of one's own actions and reactions.

However, knowing that all actions and reactions are biological does not necessarily tell one how to change them. Indeed, one might suggest that the single most important question to be asked by the mental health care researcher and provider is, what is the best way to change the brain? It is open to question whether the best way to change the brain is by using biological interventions, putting drugs into the system, using electrical devices to effect the nervous system, or neurosurgery to directly impact the brain. Psychotropic medications are the most commonly used biological intervention by far, currently recommended for almost every type of behavioral and emotional disorder. Emerging data across a number of disorders, however, suggest that at a very minimum, behavioral interventions (in contrast to biological interventions) might be just as effective, if not even more effective, in changing brain regions related to human suffering.

One must remember that human reactions are intensely specific; they involve neural firing of very complex yet specific brain cells and systems. Psychotropic medications now and into the future may not be sufficiently specific or idiographic to meet the individual's precise needs. That is, they may "wash over the brain" but not target the very specific locations of the brain related to the individual disorder in question. Once put into the system, drugs do not vary in strength and concentration over short periods of time. Behavior, moods, emotions, and thoughts do. Targeting behavior change directly—in other words, changing actions, facial expressions, posture and musculature, and thought patterns—may be a more effective way to change the brain cells and systems associated to that response system. Why not? All behavior is biology. Changing behavior is changing biology. The advantage is that the change is specific, idiographic, and time sensitive.

Clearly, there is still much research that needs to be done before these questions about the interaction between behavioral change and changes in the brain can be answered.

I am also delighted to see this book come to fruition, having anticipated its development since Allan Leventhal first approached me with the idea and I introduced the two authors in that thoroughly modern way of an e-mail exchange. The book addresses problems with the ascendance of the medical model in relation to problems in living. The claims of medication efficacy often outweigh the data. Allan Leventhal and Christopher Martell have done a wonderful job of bringing the research to the attention of the general public. What is said in this book needs to be said. They both are experienced, expert clinicians highly acclaimed by their professional peers. This book is based on their combined clinical experience as well as a wealth of research in the treatment of mental disorders and behavioral problems. You may not agree with everything they say, but you cannot fail to respect them. They may be blatant in how they present their facts but you cannot ignore what they have to say.

The authors also address the idea that in many cases depression is the result of a life lived in fear and avoidance. They suggest that therapists need to address the anxiety underlying depression that may have kept the person stuck in a spiral of sadness and regret. This is a unique and important perspective that mental health issues are related to avoidance. No matter what problematic emotion you experience, every one of them has to do with threat of some sort. Fear—threat to life. Disgust—threat to moral well-being. Empty—threat of being deprived. Jealousy—threat of losing what you have. Sadness—threat of loss and that you'll never regain. All of them have to do with threat, and they all ultimately go back to fear and fear back to avoidance.

This book is innovative and practical. Readers will find information that will empower them to make educated choices about treatment. Professionals will also find this book useful as they consider the assumptions that are made about mental illness and behavioral problems. With the increasing marketing of biological interventions and increasing marketing of psychotropic medications on television, it is good to have voices calling for balance. This book provides such a voice.

Marsha Linehan

PREFACE

If you have been feeling depressed, are worried about yourself and thinking of going to see a doctor for help, this book has been written for you. The chances are that you think there is something wrong with you and that you should be taking a pill to feel better. After all, that is what you are told in ads on television and probably have read about in many magazines and newspaper articles.

This book is aimed at informing you about what is wrong with that idea. We want you to know what alternatives you have. Our approach has been to write neither a textbook nor a self-help book, but you will find features of both in this work. In a sense, this book is a primer on depression—an objective evaluation of what has been said about it and the truth about treatments available for it.

This book is also directed at professional caregivers who either make referrals for the treatment of depression or are providing such treatment themselves, but whose busy practices may have prevented them from a careful reading of the scientific literature on the nature of depression and its treatment.

Others likely to be interested in this book are readers who are concerned about health care in the United States and how the health field has come to be dominated by the pharmaceutical industry and managed care. Given the criticisms of these industries as having placed a higher value on profits than health, there is considerable reason to question the control these companies have been accorded over our health care and to question our great reliance on them to provide this care. In this book we examine in some detail how this issue has played out in the case of the treatment of depression by antidepressant drugs.

The field of mental health, regrettably, too often has been characterized by claims that are inadequately supported by data. This is particularly the case today with respect to what has been said about the biological basis for depression and the emphasis that has been given to drug treatments for depression. We want you to know what is the actual state of our current understanding of the nature of depression, what array of treatments exist for depression, and what the scientific basis is for these treatments. Our goal is to provide you with the kind of understanding you need to make a well-informed choice when you seek help. We believe that by exposing the misinformation that exists today regarding drugs and offering you a basis for considering an alternative approach you will be in a far better position to get the best help available.

You have lived long enough to know that quick fixes, no matter how tempting they may be, are not to be trusted. Unfortunately, there has been a great deal of hype about the effectiveness of antidepressant drugs that implies that simply taking a pill will be the solution. Similarly, there is widespread belief that taking drugs is necessary because depression is caused by your biology. The fact is there is little or no scientific backing for either of these claims. The explanation of depression as something you are born with is a theory that exists without sound backing. And the science that allegedly supports the use of antidepressant drugs to correct such a biological condition is woefully weak. As the old saying goes, even though it walks like a duck and quacks like a duck, that doesn't means it is a duck. Recent careful studies have made it clear that the great bulk of the effect of these drugs is a placebo effect. They often don't work any better than a sugar pill, but you wouldn't know it because the pharmaceutical industry has spent a great deal of money to convince you of the value of their products.

There are other treatments available to you that have solid backing. These are behavioral treatments derived from many years of good research. These treatments enable you to understand how your life experiences have led you to become depressed, open up to you what you can do to overcome these negative feelings, and teach you new behaviors that become useful tools when you need them to combat feeling depressed. Instead of depending on a pill of dubious value, you will learn how you can depend on yourself when you feel bad.

You won't see advertisements for these treatments on television because professional associations such as the American Psychological Association and the National Association of Social Workers lack funding for such aggressive marketing. The idea that depression is the result of a chemical imbalance is popular because the pharmaceutical companies have large budgets for marketing. "Ask your doctor about this or that drug" is a popular expression heard on television. You will not hear an advertisement encouraging you to "ask your doctor about behavior therapy," but that is exactly the admonition we offer here.

This book has been written to give you the kind of information that we think is necessary for you to understand your situation properly. You probably will find that it is not the easiest book to read. It is not a quickie guide to happiness. A number of the chapters will require some effort on your part to become acquainted with the information you need. But that is how you can best help yourself, and it will require no more effort than you undoubtedly already put into many other important parts of your life.

In many ways this book is also about philosophy, and that regarding human behavior in particular. Although we critique the medical model currently in vogue, we recognize that our own model, although backed with significant research, may be deemed outmoded or ultimately require substantial revision. Human understanding is always evolving. It is in the spirit of hope that understanding human behavior will continue to take into account all facets of human functioning and not become reduced to the study of genes or biochemistry that we write. Our own behavioral model once focused exclusively on motor behavior, eschewing the study of anything that could not be directly observed. That, too, was reductionistic. As psychologists we enthusiastically embrace the uncertainty that remains regarding the subject of our scholarship—human beings.

Our message in this book is rooted in a respect for what you can do for yourself, just as many others have done for themselves—a message that will get reinforced by your own experience in therapy if you go through the process we recommend. We believe it is important that you have this understanding, not so that you can cure yourself (if it was that easy you probably would have done it by now), but in order for you to seek out the kind of help that will be most effective. Thus, our goal is to provide you with the understanding you need to guide you when you look for help.

The book is organized to give you a good picture of the nature of what you are dealing with when you get depressed, how to better understand what is being said about depression in the mass media and by professional caregivers, and what you can do to help yourself overcome your feelings of depression.

CHAPTER 1

SOCIETAL VIEWS OF MENTAL DISORDER

From earliest times people have attempted to comprehend the world. History is replete with explanations of the mysteries of life, many of which strike us today as foolish given our current understanding. Yet it is clear that we have always been driven to understand our world with the tools we have at our disposal. Of particular interest to humankind has been understanding occurrences that inspire awe and fear, probably because of their implications for our survival. Survival requires appraisal of the environment to detect danger, to protect ourselves from harm. Our own distress or the sight of a fellow human in distress captures our attention, as does the sight of a fellow human acting strangely. Curiosity and uneasiness about these conditions has led throughout history to attempts to explain the basis for physical and mental disorder. Religion, philosophy, and science, our most highly developed systems of thought, all concern themselves centrally with questions having to do with life and death. The wisdom of each age's most esteemed authorities was rooted in presumed expertise in these matters. Hindsight enables us to see that much of this thought was erroneous, but in their day, acting on the knowledge at their disposal, their views prevailed and dictated how society dealt with those who were afflicted.

The Medical Model

Modern science and medical treatment as we know it today is only about 150 years old. It has its roots in such figures as Galileo and

Kepler in the seventeenth century and Newton in the eighteenth century, whose work was predicated on the idea that nature is governed by natural law rather than supernatural forces. This led in the nineteenth century to medicine adopting a more naturalistic viewpoint, emphasizing observation instead of appealing to superstition. Medicine was freed from prejudices and prohibitions that had excluded experiments on the human body. In embracing the idea that the human body and its illnesses could be understood by observation and experimentation, medical scientists began applying to the arena of living organisms the empirical lessons of physics and mathematics that had produced the great advances resulting from the scientific method. Studies were conducted on the solid parts of the body via anatomical dissections, and the functioning of the body was investigated through studies of the physiology of the body's internal processes. Inventions such as the microscope and the understanding of antiseptics greatly aided advancement. The cumulative effect of this approach led to the germ theory and the comprehension that influences foreign to the normal functioning of the body, such as viruses and lesions, cause symptoms. As a result of these studies, specific treatments for illnesses, recognized through their symptoms, were developed that proved to be successful. This realization that illness is caused by a specific underlying pathological state and that successful treatment depended upon an understanding of the mechanisms governing that underlying state is called the medical model or disease model of illness.

A good example of how this evolved gradually over time by virtue of independent investigations is found in the history of how we came to understand and control diabetes. In the mid-1600s, Thomas Willis described the sweet taste of diabetic urine. In the mid-1700s, Mathew Dobson found that the sweet taste was sugar. By the mid-1800s, enough anatomical and physiological research had taken place to lead Claude Bernard to investigate the secretions of the alimentary canal and to study the pancreas and liver. He established that the liver synthesizes glycogen to keep blood glucose levels within a healthy range. In the early 1900s, Frederick Grant Banting and Charles Best discovered and isolated insulin. Bernardo Houssay then demonstrated that insulin reduced the sugar content of the blood and discovered the importance of the pituitary gland's regulating functions. This is a simplified accounting of research on a very complex disease, but it is a rough illustration of how our understanding of the nature of this disease and its current treatment, by means of monitoring blood glucose levels and insulin therapy, gradually developed.

The successful treatment of diabetes came about through a cumulative process of objective research on basic bodily functions carried out over a long period of time, eventually revealing the mechanisms involved in this disease (Andreoli, 2001). Telltale signs that had previously been treated by methods that had nothing to do with the underlying physical problems came to be understood through studies of anatomy and physiology. Such knowledge, when focused more and more specifically on the mechanisms involved, eventually led to a realization of how this disease arose and how it could be controlled. This exemplifies the medical model—comprehension of how an underlying mechanism gives rise to a disease with a pattern of symptoms—and provides a basis for a prescription to remedy the problem.

Earlier Models for Physical Disorder

A good, readable source of information about the history of medical and psychological treatment can be found in the *Cambridge Illustrated History of Medicine* (Porter, 1996). Much of the material in the next several sections of this chapter is based on that historical account, and the interested reader can find more detail by reading that volume.

From about 500 B.C. into the 1800s, from the time of the Greeks and Romans, through the Middle Ages and the Renaissance, illness was explained by a theory having to do with some form of balance or imbalance in the body. This balance had to do with elements of the universe (earth, air, fire, and water), particular fluids (humors), and certain qualities (such as hot and cold, sweet and sour). The theory held that the body should not become too cold or hot or too wet or dry. Disease was believed to be the result of an excess or deficiency of the wet and dry, hot and cold humors.

Hippocrates (460–377 B.C.) is regarded as the father of medicine because of his advocating the experimental method, his rejection of superstitious views of illness and sorcery, and his admonition to help, not harm, the patient. He emphasized the importance of observation and experimentation in understanding illness. Nevertheless, in the absence of knowledge of the functioning of the human body, Hippocrates explained disease according to the theoretical model of humors and engaged in treatment practices that were, in fact, harmful. Galen (129–216 A.D.), another major figure in the history of medicine, fine-tuned this theory of humors and elaborated the treatment practices of the day that were derived from it. Treatment was based on the notion that health depended upon the body functioning efficiently in processing and evacuating what it took in. Food and drink were identified as the ingredients necessary to fuel life. Blood-letting, emetics, "sweats," and, most important, purges were treatments offered for maintaining or regaining health by facilitating the flow of the humors in the blood. Laxatives of mercury and lead came to be used for purgatives because there was no understanding that these metals were poisonous. Blood-letting caused people to become anemic, and purgatives drained the body of fluids and electrolytes important to health (Singer & Underwood, 1962). Despite the unhelpful effects of such treatments, these highly accepted, widespread practices were the medical treatments of choice for 20 centuries, from the time of Hippocrates to as late as the middle of the nineteenth century, when research in chemistry, anatomy, and physiology finally made it clear that the theory was false, the treatments useless at best and generally detrimental to health. Whatever good resulted from these treatment efforts would have to be attributable to a placebo effect.

Medical practice during these times also frequently made use of drugs. In the first century A.D., Pedanius Dioscorides produced a five-volume work on medicinal herbs. These books, which were translated into many languages, were called *De Materia Medica*. Although we now know that only 44 of the 500 recommended drugs have any value, *De Materia Medica* was the definitive authority on medicines for 1,500 years.

In addition to these medical explanations of illness and medical prescriptions for the remedy of illness dating from ancient times, there have also been powerful explanations and prescriptions derived from religious beliefs. For most of recorded history, these ideas dictated medical treatment. The Old Testament of the Bible (Leviticus 13:2) explains illness as the result of moral lapses as well as physical causes. Illness was viewed as the physical manifestation of a spiritual malaise. An example is found in the writings on leprosy, which at the time was the name given to a variety of skin disorders, the treatment for which was isolation from others.

Playing on the linguistic similarity of the Hebrew word for "leper" and the Hebrew phrase for "one who gossips," the rabbis considered leprosy to be a punishment for the sins of slander and malicious gossip (Lev. R. 16:1). They taught that gossip is like leprosy because it is highly contagious. One infected person can spread malicious rumor to many others. Seven types of antisocial behavior that God punishes were designated: "haughty eyes, a lying tongue, hands that shed innocent blood in secret, a mind that hatches evil, feet quick to do wrong, a witness who testifies falsely, and one who incites brothers to quarrel" (Prov. 6:16–19). Those types of behavior share the attribute of being difficult to prove or punish in a court of law. Thus, God exacts punishment in a variety of appropriate ways: "As your rumors separated husband from wife and brother from brother, you will now be separated from all human contact. The Midrash adduces proof texts to show that people guilty of these misdeeds were punished with leprosy" (Etz Hayim, 2001).

Papyri in ancient Egypt (1570 B.C.) attributed illness to a demon having entered a person's body. The Greeks erected shrines to Asclepius, the god of healing, and these shrines were the sites of treatment. The "patient" slept in the temple and in the morning recounted his dreams to a priest, whose interpretation of the dreams was the basis for treatment.

The Medieval Period and the Renaissance

Medicine in Europe developed within a church-established conceptualization of illness. The biblical story of Adam and Eve's transgressions in the Garden of Eden was cited as the basis for sin, misery, illness, and death. The flesh was regarded as weak and corruptible in contrast to the soul, which was immortal. Thus, priests were regarded as higher authorities than doctors in explaining illness. Favorite treatments were prayer, self-flagellation, fasting, and chastity. Healing rituals were devised and saints became famous for their healing powers. There were pilgrimages to holy places, and certain people came to be regarded as having special powers as healers. For example, Bridget Bostock claimed to cure illnesses with holy spittle, and Valentine Greatrakes healed by the laying on of the hands.

Nevertheless, a power struggle and an ambiguous and conflicted division of labor existed between priests and doctors. The Fourth Lateran Council (1215) in Rome prohibited clerics from blood-letting and surgery. Doctors were given the job of treating illness, but their authority was limited by the prevailing religious views. A person's illness was understood to be attributable to three possible causes: disease, malingering, or possession by an evil spirit. It was the doctor's job to make this differential diagnosis. Whenever the futility of medical practice was exposed by epidemics and plagues, the church reclaimed its authority in addressing illness, declaring that these mass illnesses were punishments from God requiring some form of atonement. The Black Death (bubonic plague) in the fourteenth century was a time when the church's authority overtook that of doctors. Some communities, on the advice of doctors, sought to isolate the sick by locking city gates, imposing quarantines, and closing public markets. Priests, however, condemned these efforts as impious and stated that they were medically of no value. In a confrontation during the Renaissance, the church excommunicated all the members of the Florentine Health Board. There was widespread belief on both sides that these epidemics were the work of the devil, the only difference being how best to respond.

Some commentators took exception to these ideas. Leonardo da Vinci (1452–1519) questioned the medical views of Galen and the church's views, but his writings on this subject were unknown until much later. In the seventeenth century, the philosophers Descartes and Hobbes were critical of ideas that attributed illness to other than natural causes. They argued for disease to be subjected to empirical study, viewing nature as like a machine that was governed by fundamental, unchangeable, natural laws. But it took another 200 years for this paradigm shift to occur in the mid-1800s.

The Medical Model Applied to Mental Disorder

In the twentieth century, the medical model was extended to apply to mental disorder as well as to physical disorder. According to the application of this model to mental disorder, an individual's behavior is deemed to be diseased, abnormal, or disordered because of the existence of an underlying cause, which may be psychological or physical, depending upon the particular theory being espoused.

Psychoanalysis represented a psychological expression of the medical model. Psychoanalytic theory postulates that symptoms are simply by-products of an underlying hidden cause stemming from experiences in early childhood that have produced unconscious psychic conflicts. Treating the person's behavior instead of these underlying psychic conflicts was condemned as superficial, useless, even harmful, and doomed to failure. The evidence for this proposition was given in case reports. No empirically based outcome studies of the efficacy of psychoanalysis have been conducted, although it is still practiced throughout the world.

More popular, currently, are biological explanations for mental disorder based upon the medical model. These theories hold that mental disorder is the result of an imbalance in brain chemistry; for example, an insufficiency of the neurotransmitter serotonin (a biogenic amine) is postulated to explain depression. Other neurotransmitters are cited to explain schizophrenia, eating disorders, alcoholism, violence, and shyness. Administering a chemical boost to the deficient neu-rotransmitter is the treatment of choice. However, as is the case with psychoanalysis, none of these claims is based upon objective findings that establish the presumed mechanisms involved in causation. They are based upon extrapolations from studies that have found that the administration of medications to increase these neurotransmitters are accompanied by a reduction of some of the symptoms for some people, with no substantiated mechanism having been established to account for the effects. In the absence of any demonstration of direct linkages, the interpretation of these studies is open to considerable ques-tion given the complexity of the connection between human behavior and human biology. H. S. Akiskal (1995) in a major medical textbook in psychiatry states that, "despite three decades of extensive research and indirect evidence, however, it has not been proved that a deficiency or excess of biogenic amines in specific brain structures is necessary or sufficient for the occurrence of mood disorders" (p. 1076).

Without a true understanding based upon objective research of the underlying mechanisms, theories and prescriptions are merely guess-work no matter how they may be dressed up with scientific language. Moreover, treatments for depression (and other disorders) based upon the neurotransmitter theory, and based upon the medical model, have proven to be of limited value, as is discussed in succeeding chap-ters in this book. This is not to say that the brain is not involved in psychological disorders. Akiskal, who reviewed studies of biological etiology of depression, states that "evidence of midbrain disturbance argues for considering clinical depression a legitimate illness" (p. 1076). Note, however, that he states that such a conclusion may be considered; it is not an established fact by any means and there is much future research to be done. The main point to remember is that, although the study of biochemical processes in the brain as they relate to human behavior is interesting and will in all likelihood continue to increase our understanding of human functioning, the facts do not equal the claims made regarding depression (or other problems such as social anxiety, for example) resulting from a "chemical imbalance in the brain." Labeling depression an illness or disease is more in the realm of opinion than fact.

Again, the basic premise of the medical model is that there are underlying causes for behaviors that are viewed as symptoms. Diabe-tes is an often-cited metaphor in explaining the biological basis for depression. It is argued that just like the fatigue or frequent urination of the diabetic is the symptom of the underlying disease, the sadness, lethargy, and hopelessness of the depressed person are symptoms of an underlying biochemical or psychological process. Clearly, the medical model is to be much preferred to ancient theories of possession by evil spirits or divine curses. It is a model that, when applied to physical disorders, has allowed humans to enjoy long life and relative good health that our ancestors could only dream of. However, the proof of the medical model when applied to mental disorder is equivocal and relies on a philosophical idea regarding humans that can easily become reductionistic, losing sight of social and environmental factors that interplay with behavior and biochemistry.

A Learning or Functional Model

The medical model is not the only potentially useful model that may be derived from scientific research. An alternative model is one derived from a great deal of behavioral research. This learning, or functional, model holds a great deal of promise because it has been formulated on the basis of controlled laboratory studies and has been demonstrated to account far more successfully for behavior, whether it is normal or abnormal. A comment from Akiskal in the Kaplan and Saddock text states a possible connection between a behavioral model and a biological model: "by focusing on reward mechanisms, the behavioral model provides a conceptual bridge between purely psychological and emerging biological conceptualizations of depression" (1995, p. 1075). This learning model will be presented in more detail in Chapters 4 and 5.

The field of mental health is still very young, with much more unknown than known. The nature-nurture controversy is still very much alive. Scientific literature found in leading psychological and medical journals usually arrives at the conclusion of an interaction of multiple factors, but popular opinion and the marketing of pharmaceutical products present the medical illness model as the exclusive explanation of mental disorder as if it is an undisputed fact. As we shall see, there is much reason to question this viewpoint.

The History of Attention to Mental Disorder

Societal attention to mental disorder also stretches far back in history with a similar pattern of theories and practices of little or no value to the patient until recent times. The generally accepted starting point for the history of society's attention to mental disorder was with the Greeks writing about madness. Homer's writings explained mental disorder as occurring when the gods removed a person's rationality. As was the case in addressing physical disorders, the early Greeks looked to interpretations of patients' dreams in temples of Asclepius to prescribe a cure. Later, humans were seen by the Greeks as unique in having a psyche, which enabled the states of consciousness and self-reflection. Madness was explained as the product of a conflicted mind, as exemplified in conflicts of love versus hate and duty versus desire. Socrates, Plato, and Aristotle spoke of reason as the ideal state and mental disorder as irrationality. Mental processes were regarded as the province of philosophers and theologians rather than of physicians (Foucault, 1965).

Hippocrates argued that psychological problems were the province of medicine. Calling for mental disorder to be studied objectively, his writings are filled with psychological descriptions of depression, postpartum psychoses, phobias, and memory disturbances. However, as was the case in his writings on physical disorders, despite his emphasis on the search for natural causes, his explanations for mental disorder and the treatments he recommended reflected the ignorance of his times. He believed that intelligence and affect were derived from inhaled air. In subscribing to the theory of humors, he believed that bile played a dominant role in mental disorder: too much yellow bile in the brain causes anxiety and too much black bile causes depression. He explained mania as the result of excessive warmth and a condition of dampness in the brain. He believed epilepsy to be caused by spring weather. And, as was the case with physical disorder, his treatments for such disorders were bleeding, purging, fasting, drugs (most of which we now know to be useless), and rest.

Seven centuries later, Galen (around 200 A.D.) elaborated upon these Hippocratic ideas regarding mental disorder. Galen paid particular attention to the central nervous system as explanatory of mental disorder, describing the brain as central. He believed in a theory of temperaments that was derived from the humors. Each of the four humors of blood, phlegm, yellow bile, and black bile was considered to be associated with a different temperament. Elaborating on earlier Greek ideas, he postulated various souls that governed bodily functions, writing of an "animal soul" that directed sensation and feeling and an "intellectual soul" governing mental functions.

For the Greeks and Romans, over the course of many centuries mental disorder was an amalgam of ideas, some having to do with moral/psychological lapses, others having to do with these concepts of the humors as associated with physical disorder. Attention to mental disorder required taking control of the emotions, adopting a virtuous way of life, and purging as recommended by Hippocrates and Galen.

These ideas continued during the Middle Ages and Renaissance, during which there was an increase in attention to such behavior by the church. For the church, mental disorder was the result of a conflict between God and Satan battling for the soul. Therefore, the diagnosis and treatment of mental disorder was assigned to the clergy rather than to medical doctors. Medicine was limited to treating physical ailments. Prayer and fasting were the preferred remedies for mental disorder at first. For more than 1,000 years, demonology provided a structure that dominated the explanation of mental disorder and with it came harsher methods. In the thirteenth century, flagellation was the most common treatment employed to rid a person of demons. In the fifteenth century, the Inquisition introduced a document entitled the *Maleus Maleficarum* (the Witches Hammer). It was all about how witches came to exist, their activities, and what needed to be done to get rid of them and the devil empowering them. Mental disorder was seen as religious madness of diabolical origin, the work of witches and heretics. Burning at the stake was the usual treatment (Zilboorg & Henry, 1941). Doctors, who usually also were priests, were recruited to comment on the activities of the devil, and a legal system was established to prosecute witches and the possessed. For more than 200 years, cruelty was common, justified as a means to exorcise demons.

The Beginning of Reforms

It was not until the seventeenth century that these ideas and practices began to come into disrepute. By that time, witch-hunts had gotten so out of hand that authorities took measures to put an end to them. Those who had been labeled as witches were described instead as deluded, and demonism was condemned. Benjamin Rush (1745–1813), generally regarded as the father of psychiatry, championed the idea that mental disorder was a pathological condition of the mind rather than a product of some supernatural invasion. He theorized a more naturalistic, physical explanation for mental disorder as the need for better blood circulation to the brain. However, his treatment methods continued to emphasize blood-letting, emetics, and purgatives as the means of promoting improved blood circulation.

By the eighteenth century, demonology was out of favor as an explanation of mental disorder, replaced by a theory of problems in the sensory and nervous systems. Doctors began speaking of "nerves," and the term "neurosis" came into use to denote a physical lesion presumed present in the nervous system (Porter, 1996). Later, the term "neurosis" was redefined as a nonspecific anxiety state distinguished from "psychosis," which denoted a more severe condition. This new viewpoint on mental disorder led to the development of institutions to house the mentally disordered who previously had been hidden away in their homes by their families. Now they were sent to institutions along with others who failed to comply with societal norms, such as the homeless and criminals. These institutions were dreadful places. The patients were often kept in chains and accorded no dignity, often objects of derision. In the beginning, the older treatments of bloodletting and purgatives continued along with new treatment techniques that were developed, such as chairs spun at high speeds and cold water douches, which were designed to shock and tranquilize patients, making them more amenable to reason.

The Development of Psychological Approaches

By the mid-1800s, blood-letting no longer was condoned. Great reforms took place as psychological approaches were developed as the primary means of treatment. Pierre Janet (1859–1947) conceived of neurosis as an inborn weakness of the nervous system. His treatment, however, was not based on physical measures, but was more psychological in nature. As such, it was a precursor to Freud. Psychiatrists talked with patients to discuss their thoughts, met with relatives, and arranged cheerful surroundings for hospitalized patients. The physical restraints were removed, humanitarian practices were adopted, and stages were devised in the care of the institutionalized that moved them with improvement toward greater contact with the outside world. Work as a form of therapy was instituted. A psychological theory of treatment arose that focused on the doctor-patient relationship, which was now fully the responsibility of psychiatrists. The doctor sought charisma as an important element in promoting power and efficacy. Psychological tactics were pursued that would undermine the irrationalities of the mentally disordered state. These patients were now viewed as immature children whose cure was to be found in teaching them how to think and feel properly as adults.

In Europe and the United States, the popularity of these ideas resulted in a rapid rise in the number of persons institutionalized for mental disorder (Foucault, 1965). For example, in the United States in 1850, 5,000 people were in such hospitals; in 1904, 150,000; by 1950, 500,000. As conditions became more crowded, treatment efforts dwindled and often disappeared entirely. Patients received housing and little else. By the turn of the twentieth century, it became clear that the great results psychiatrists had claimed for their methods were nonexistent. Not only was there a significant increase in the number of chronic cases showing no improvement, but some critics began complaining that these human warehouses worsened the problem.

The Ascendancy of Physical Approaches

Souring on the prevalent psychological methods, medical scientists began searching for an organic cause for mental disorder and began employing physical methods of treatment. Insulin shock and electroshock therapies were devised, along with prefrontal lobotomy. Drugs such as barbiturates came into increased usage. Kraepelin (1856–1926) in 1883 attributed all mental disorder to biological factors and divided mental disorder into the curable (those caused by environmental conditions) and the incurable (those caused by constitutional determinants). His nosology of two major categories of psychoses, dementia praecox (soon renamed schizophrenia by Bleuler) and manic depressive psychosis, remains the major basis for classification to this day. Kraepelin and others suggested a number of possible organic factors as the cause of mental disorders: heredity, toxins (alcohol, narcotics, metal poisoning), brain disease, infections, circulatory problems, and brain pathology. Kraepelin sought to establish a system that specified certain symptoms distinguishing one mental disease from another. Syndromes were labeled when symptoms clustered, but unfortunately his search for distinct clusters of symptoms that would distinguish one disorder from another failed. There was much overlap in the symptoms from one disorder to another.

A great effort ensued to identify an organic basis for the various mental disorders. The search for such underlying physical causes found some confirmation in the findings of Kraft-Ebing (1840–1903), who discovered the relationship of general paresis to syphilis, and the work of Korsakov (1854–1900), who established the relationship between some psychoses and excessive alcohol consumption. However, these were atypical mental disorders and, despite vigorous continuing efforts to discover organic causes for the more commonly seen mental disorders, no other discoveries were made.

Continued Swings of the Pendulum

The pendulum soon swung back to psychological methods. Early in the twentieth century, Sigmund Freud (1856–1939) began developing his theory and practice of psychoanalysis. His theory held that mental disorder is due to repression that is governed by the unconscious mind, fueled by psychic energy (libido), and expressed in particular behaviors in stages during childhood of psychosexual development. Mastery of internal versus external demands by means of a pleasure principle versus a reality principle was viewed as central to mental disorder. The theory was elaborate and intellectually compelling, with its features explained and justified by means of case reports (anecdotal evidence) that spelled out a dynamic theory of personality and therapy. After an initial period of skepticism, Freud's system became highly influential, emerging as the primary basis for explaining mental disorder. Psychological treatment methods derived from Freud's views dominated psychiatry from early in the twentieth century until the 1980s. Its popularity owed no small part of its success to its appeal to writers, for whom it was a treasure trove of interesting ideas for character development in novels. Unfortunately, the therapy was lengthy, expensive, and met with mixed results at best.

Within this same time period, there were developed other briefer, less costly forms of psychotherapy, some of which were based on the psychoanalytic theoretical model, while others were derived from different models. These treatments showed some promise and became popular. Mental disorder was conceptualized as on a continuum with normal behavior; that is, a difference in degree, not kind. Treatment for many mental disorders on an outpatient basis became more commonplace, and the stigma was significantly reduced. Many people clearly benefited from supportive and educational elements in these treatments. However, the mechanisms underlying these gains remained unknown.

A particular school of therapy, behavioral psychology, generated by psychological research primarily into the process of learning, developed new treatment methods that not only were found to be effective for specific factors (indeed, their success led to some revisions in the diagnostic manual for mental disorders), but postulated mechanisms for these results that were derived from behavioral research. These treatments and their theoretical basis, which is the primary subject matter of this book, have not been given the recognition they deserve. As a result, many people in need are not getting help that is now available. Chapters 5 and 6 describe behavioral treatments in some detail.

Psychoanalysis, however, was the treatment most people thought of in the twentieth century when they thought of psychological treatment. The costly, largely inadequate results with the psychoanalytically derived methods, together with economic problems for the profession of psychiatry, resulted in a return by psychiatrists late in the century to physical methods of treatment, based upon a theory of brain chemistry. Thus, the pendulum has now swung in the opposite direction. These physical methods have predominated to the present time as psychiatrists have adopted a new biological viewpoint, relegating psychological explanations to a secondary status. This biological trend was immensely augmented by the development of drugs by the pharmaceutical industry that have been alleged to alleviate a biochemical basis for mental disorder.

It is important to reiterate that, while medicine was making great advances in the twentieth century in ferreting out underlying causes for physical disorders, few unequivocal findings were discovered with respect to mental disorder. Those seemingly positive reports that appeared soon proved to be unsubstantiated. As a result, in contrast to physical medicine where diagnosis was related to an objectively derived etiology that dictated a specific treatment method, when it came to mental disorder, diagnosis and the great bulk of treatment has had no such objective underpinning. This has been true of the psychological theories in vogue and it is true of the biological theories, despite vigorous efforts and increasingly sophisticated means of studying physical factors that might yield an explanation of the etiology of mental disorder.

Economics and Professions

The middle of the twentieth century witnessed the emergence of clinical psychology. The need during World War II for large numbers of mental health personnel led to the military training of psychologists, principally to do diagnostic testing. Prior to the war, psychologists had developed tests for measuring intelligence, personality, and brain injury that were very useful in the diagnosis and treatment of military personnel. With the blossoming of interest in mental health following the war, departments of psychology at universities across the country began educating a far larger number of psychology graduate students. Unlike psychiatrists who were trained in university professional programs (medical schools) and earned medical degrees, psychologists received their training in graduate schools whose core curriculum emphasized research methodology leading to the Doctor of Philosophy (Ph.D.) degree.

Psychology departments had been educating psychologists as researchers since the late 1800s and a good deal of basic and applied research had been accomplished by the mid-1900s, but the great influx of new students, many of whom were as interested in applied research as they were in basic research, led to the rapid development of the field of clinical psychology. The research efforts of this new cadre of mental health personnel not only began to provide a scientific base for understanding and controlling human behavior, it also produced a desire by psychologists for recognition as an independent profession within which they could provide treatments based on their training and research. Although the fields of psychology, sociology, and social work had much to say about human problems, psychiatry maintained a monopoly on psychotherapy until the early 1960s (Valenstein, 1998). Non-physicians were prevented from attending psychoanalytic institutes, and psychologists or social workers practicing psychotherapy were accused of practicing medicine without a license. In the 1950s, conflict emerged when psychologists mounted an effort for legislation to grant state licensure in order to free them of control by psychiatry. Despite bitter opposition from medicine and psychiatry that psychotherapy was medical practice that required medical training, the growing power of psychology together with the predominance of Freud's psychological theory of mental disorder enabled psychologists to succeed in gaining independent status.

Another series of battles took place in the 1960s regarding recognition for insurance reimbursement, a key issue for pursuing private practice successfully. Psychology prevailed in making the case that a psychologist's patient was equally entitled to such coverage. Insurance companies opened up third-party reimbursement to psychologists, and later to social workers and some counselors. Psychiatry lost its hold on the mental health field, and the privileges of the medical degree began slipping away. Turf battles have ensued among psychologists, social workers, nurse practitioners, and others, and all of the professional fields have been guilty of trying to protect their domains of practice from others, usually with little, if any, evidence that other like-minded professionals cannot perform the duties with equal competence. The turf wars between psychiatry and psychology erupted again in the 1970s with the advent of legislation to grant privileged communication to patients in psychotherapy. Psychiatrists argued that this protection of confidentiality should be extended only to their patients, but state legislation was passed nationwide based upon the function being performed (the psychotherapeutic relationship) rather than the discipline of the practitioner, on the grounds that the privilege was the property of the patient.

During this same period of time, psychologists were doing objective research on the nature of the psychotherapeutic process (Rogers, 1951), which was being transmitted in the training of psychologists. Graduate study in clinical psychology was based on a scientist-practitioner model (Raimy, 1950) and emphasized research in human behavior as well as training in psychotherapy. Psychologists spent their energies studying the science of human behavior, understanding what behaviors were statistically normal, how behavior was learned and modified, and applying this scientific knowledge to behavior change.

The Crisis for Psychiatry and the Biological Revolution

For a long time psychiatrists were viewed with suspicion by the rest of medicine as not being real doctors. In fact, for a period of time in the 1970s the medical internship year was eliminated for those specializing in psychiatry. By the 1980s fewer and fewer medical students were pursuing psychiatry as a specialty. Psychiatrists found themselves increasingly rejected by their patients in favor of other practitioners, and many psychiatrists grew concerned that the continued existence of psychiatry as a medical specialty was endangered. An article in the *New York Times* in 1982 described the situation:

> American psychiatrists are increasingly distressed because they believe too few medical school students are being attracted to the profession to keep psychiatry vital and to meet the nation's mental health needs.... From 1970 to 1980 the percentage of medical students drawn to psychiatry fell from above 11 percent to less than half that proportion.... [E]fforts are underway to raise the scientific quality of psychiatric education in medical schools, to promote recruitment into the field and to improve the public's esteem for psychiatry.... [C]areer interest in psychiatry has plunged just when many medical experts say the nation is facing a shortage of psychiatrists.... The reluctance of medical students

to enter the field is especially galling and demoralizing to psychiatrists who remember their discipline as the fastest-growing medical specialty in the heady years after World War II.... What the waning enthusiasm for their field has forced psychiatrists to confront more directly is their low position on the medical profession's totem pole.... The students have been disconcerted by the large influx of people into the therapy business from a variety of other backgrounds—including psychology, social work and pastoral counseling. Not only do these often highly trained professionals offer economic competition, but they can make the student wonder why an arduous medical education is needed to do similar work.... Dr. Stuart C. Yudolfsky, vice chairman of the psychiatry department at Columbia University's College of Physicians and Surgeons, said, "There was too much emphasis on social theory rather than on the biological and pharmacological triumphs in psychiatry." (Nelson, 1982)

Although at this time there existed within psychiatry a minority who had continued to advocate a biological viewpoint, they tended to be psychiatrists who treated only very serious cases or served as adjuncts to patients seen by others (including psychiatrists) for psychotherapy. Most psychiatrists treated a general clientele and considered the use of drugs as secondary in their treatment, which was based on a psychological (psychoanalytic) point of view. Now, however, with the field of psychiatry in economic trouble, the biologically oriented psychiatrists took control as the field sought to remake itself and utilize medical expertise in the treatment of a broader array of human problems. They argued vigorously and successfully for a return to an organic orientation and for the importance of adopting a single voice on this issue. As one writer put it in the *American Journal of Psychiatry* in 1981, "There are two political influences of great power: insurers and bureaucrats want clear definitions and agreed-upon entities. Moreover, psychiatry wants to speak with a unified voice not only to secure their support but to buttress its own position against numerous other mental health professionals seeking patients and prestige" (Havens, 1981).

Central to this transformation of the field of psychiatry was redirection of the research effort at the National Institute of Mental Health (NIMH), founded in 1948 as a part of the National Institutes of Health (NIH) to be the prime agency for funding research on mental disorder. Research at the NIMH had been under two umbrellas: one to support grants for pharmacological research and one to support grants for psychotherapy research. A reorganization in the early 1980s simply eliminated the latter branch. Clinical trials according to diagnostic categories treated via drugs was firmly established.

Diagnosis

Given the prominence that was accorded to diagnosis by the NIMH, let's take a look at the diagnostic system for classifying mental disorder. The official diagnostic manual for mental disorders is published by the American Psychiatric Association. Entitled *Diagnostic and Statistical Manual of Mental Disorders* (DSM), it was first published in 1952 and has gone through a number of subsequent revisions—DSM-II in 1968, DSM-III in 1980, DSM-IIIR in 1987, DSM-IV in 1994, and DSM-IV TR in 2000. The first two editions were modest in size, having about 150 pages and listing about 100 mental disorders. Numerous studies of the DSM demonstrated the scientific unreliability of the system. Not only was diagnostic agreement weak for major categories (for example, psychosis versus neurosis), when it came to a specific diagnosis for a particular patient, agreements were reported in, at best, only about half the cases. Since the generally accepted statistical standard for individual prediction (in this case individual differential diagnosis) is .90 or better, correlations of .20 and .50 plainly are highly unsatisfactory. DSM-I and DSM-II failed to meet the most basic requirement of a classification system—that is, that different observers come to the same conclusion about what is being observed. Most importantly from a substantive standpoint, without reliability you cannot have a valid instrument.

The American Psychiatric Association appointed a psychiatrist to direct task forces to produce a new and more respectable DSM. This effort led to the publication of DSM-III and DSM-IIIR, which were aimed primarily at correcting the problems with reliability. In addition, beginning with DSM-III, the new editions also aimed to replace psychological characterizations of mental disorder with biological assumptions, based on the claim that this made for a more scientific taxonomy. According to Gerald Klerman, who at the time was the psychiatrist holding the highest position in the federal government, "The decision of the American Psychiatric Association to develop DSM-III and to promulgate its use represents a significant reaffirmation on the part American psychiatry to its medical identity and its commitment to scientific medicine" (Klerman, 1984, p. 539).

Revisions of the DSM require approval from the membership of the American Psychiatric Association. The revision was presented at the annual meeting of the American Psychiatric Association in 1979, where it was approved enthusiastically by the assembly. The strategy that had been adopted for the revision was described as one that enabled an increase in the objectivity of the system by means of a checklist of symptoms deemed necessary to arrive at a diagnosis. The manual was much longer: it had swollen to 900 pages covering 227 diagnoses, more than doubling the number of diagnoses over the previous system. DSM-IV increased the total number of diagnoses over DSM-III by more than 25 percent to almost 300 diagnoses.

However, the reliability issue was supposed to be key. The field trials were described by the director of the project as having unequivocally established the reliability of the new edition by demonstrating a very significant improvement over previous editions. He proclaimed DSM-III's reliability to be "extremely good" (Hyler, Williams, & Spitzer, 1982). Other prominent psychiatrists joined in to give DSM-III hearty endorsement as a major improvement. Gerald Klerman, head of the Alcohol, Drug, and Mental Health Administration, made the sweeping statement, "In principle, the problem of reliability has been solved" (Klerman, 1986, p. 25). Since the late 1980s, Kirk and Kutchins have been studying the work that was done in revising the DSM and have provided several excellent critiques of this process (most notably, Kirk & Kutchins, 1992; Kutchins & Kirk, 1997). They report that the claims for reliability of DSM-III were so well accepted that, prior to 1992, there was no thorough review of the data on which the claims of greater reliability were based (Kirk & Kutchins, 1992).

> By developing a massive superstructure consisting of dozens of committees and involving hundreds of participants, the [DSM] Task Force created the illusion that the development of the manual was the result of an enormous research effort. Despite the widespread participation of psychiatrists and other mental health professionals, actual decisions were made by a small group of participants in the Task Force. Research, including the data generated from a large federally supported study, was used selectively to support the goals of the Task Force and to undermine the objections of their opponents. (Kirk & Kutchins, 1992, p. 14)

In carrying out the field trials, the standard for reliability that was chosen was a correlation of .70, not the usually expected .90. Moreover, an unfamiliar statistic was used that made interpretation confusing even to readers familiar with correlational statistics (Kirk & Kutchins, 1992). Against this criterion, in the field trials that were conducted (which were supported by the NIMH), when it came to classifying according to Axis I (that is, the major disorders such as schizophrenia, mood disorders, anxiety disorders, and so on), only 31 of 80 correlations met the criterion of .70. When it came to children and adolescents, the results were worse: only 8 of the 24 correlations met the criterion. For Axis II (personality disorders), only 1 of 7 correlations met the criterion (Kirk & Kutchins, 1992). More pertinent to clinical situations is the reliability of judgments concerning specific diagnoses within these major categories. When it came to such specific diagnoses (for example, the various diagnoses included under anxiety disorders), it was found that the researchers had engaged in a curious practice when tallying the data. Diagnostic agreement was considered "perfect" if the various diagnoses were in the same class. For example, if one clinician diagnosed a case as agoraphobia with panic attacks and another clinician diagnosed that case as obsessive-compulsive disorder, they were rated as being in perfect agreement because both diagnoses fell under the heading of anxiety disorders. In addition, results are reported within DSM-III for only 16 of the more than 200 such possible diagnoses. This, in itself, is remarkable since diagnosis at this level was the prime concern regarding the unreliability in DSM-I and II; this kind of diagnosis in the real world determines the course of treatment and insurance coverage. For these 16 diagnoses, only 9 of the 26 correlations met the selected criterion. Kirk and Kutchins conclude: "The DSM revolution in reliability is a revolution in rhetoric, not in reality" (Kirk & Kutchins, 1997, p. 53).

Pharmaceutical companies have contributed directly to the development of the DSM. More people being diagnosed with mental disorder is good for business. The director of the task forces to revise the DSM was part of a group that developed an instrument named Prime-MD that was funded by Pfizer, which holds the copyright to it. It is a 26-item self-administered checklist for use by patients of primary care physicians to diagnose a wide range of disorders, including anxiety conditions, depression, substance abuse or alcoholism, and so forth.

> The physician, using a companion DSM-based instrument, can make a psychiatric diagnosis in an average of only eight minutes and can then, presumably, prescribe medication or make a referral to a psychiatrist.... Thus, this new checklist, called Prime-MD, is the Alaskan pipeline for the pharmaceuticals, a method for gaining direct access to an immense new market. (Kutchins & Kirk, 1997, p. 13)

Since the publication of DSM-III in 1980 there has been no published study attesting to improved reliability of the DSM in clinical settings. No reliability studies were conducted by the American Psychiatric Association or by the DSM-III Task Force after it was published. In fact, the issue of reliability wasn't even mentioned in DSM-IIIR. The American Psychiatric Association had a grant from the MacArthur Foundation during the production of DSM-IV to study reliability in clinical settings. The results, while obtained, were never published. Another study, whose primary investigator was the DSM Task Force director's wife and is a professor at Columbia University, involved intensive training of mental health professionals internationally and the diagnosis of 600 patients. Kutchins and Kirk report that the results were

> not different from those statistics achieved in the 1950s and 1960s—and in some cases worse.... What this study demonstrated was that even when experienced clinicians with special training and supervision are asked to use DSM and make a diagnosis, they frequently disagree, even though the standards for defining agreement are very generous. (Kutchins & Kirk, 1997, pp. 52–53)

A recent review of the history of the DSM included statements from the two psychiatrists most responsible for producing DSM-III and DSM-IV. When questioned about reliability, Spitzer (the director of the DSM-III editions) is reported to have answered, "To say that we've solved the reliability problem is just not true...if you are in a situation with a general clinician it's certainly not very good" (Spiegel, 2005, p. 63). Frances (the director of the DSM-IV editions) was reported to have stated, "Without reliability the system is completely random, and the diagnoses means almost nothing—maybe worse than nothing because they're false labeling. You're better off not having a diagnostic system" (Spiegel, 2005, p. 58). Unfortunately, what was written in the late 1960s remains true. There is so much overlap in the definitions of different disorders that a label attached by one professional is as influential to another professional as the behavior of the patient (Ullman & Krasner, 1969). And as the editors of the *Cambridge History of Medicine* state:

> A glance at successive editions of the Diagnostic and Statistical Manual (DSM), the profession's diagnostic handbook produced by the American Psychiatric Association, shows just how fluid the characterization of mental illness continues to be. DSM reveals a proliferation of different, often incompatible terminologies, some disappearing and reappearing from edition to edition. (Porter, 1996, p. 300)

Ross, a psychiatrist who has written on the subject of the DSM, has stated:

> [The] political decisions in DSM-IV ... refute the proposition that biological psychiatrists are good, scientific diagnosticians, because I know

the history first hand.... It might be objected that the DSM-IV system
and biological psychiatry are two separate things, and that problems
with DSM-IV cannot necessarily be blamed on bioreductionists.
Although this is true in theory, in reality the system is driven by bioreductionist assumptions and ideology. (Ross & Pam, 1995, p. 125)

By "bioreductionist" the author means reducing all explanations of
etiology to biological phenomena. The danger of reductionism is present in all explanatory models, including behaviorism, as is discussed in
later chapters. Suffice it here to point out that biological psychiatry is
one form of reductionism that does not have a clear and complete picture of human behavior, although marketing promotions strongly
suggest that "biochemical imbalances" are at the root of most, if not
all, psychological problems.

The DSM has failed to satisfy the most basic scientific requirements
for a classification instrument. As a diagnostic tool, the DSM is a far
cry from the substantive value of diagnostic guides at hand for diagnosing physical disorder. If we turn back to where this discussion of
diagnosis began—that is, with the decision by the NIMH to require
that research proposals focus on DSM diagnosis—the fallacy of this
policy is obvious. Nevertheless, in the 1980s research designed to
(a) study the use of drugs to (b) treat various DSM diagnoses was
adopted as the research strategy of choice, and continues to be so, for
the National Institute of Mental Health.

The Power of Money

The question of how much influence economic factors have had in
guiding the positions adopted by psychiatry with respect to explaining
depression as of biological origin, advocating pharmacological treatment for depression, emphasizing research support for pharmacological studies, and its philosophy in revising the DSM, is, of course, open
to debate. However, there certainly is some history of professional
organizations apparently being swayed by economic forces. As a likely
example, before 1951, for 50 years, absent government regulation
requiring the pharmaceutical industry to prove the worth of its products, the American Medical Association (AMA) had taken responsibility for determining which drugs were useful and which were not. The
AMA, through its own laboratory, certified drugs and published an
annual review detailing worthwhile medications. Without the AMA's
seal of approval, drug companies were prohibited from advertising in

the AMA's journal. Few drugs required a prescription, however. In 1951, to protect the public, a federal law was passed that greatly expanded the number of drugs obtainable only with a doctor's prescription. Drug companies thereafter adopted a marketing strategy of spending money to influence doctors and their organizations. Whereas in 1950 the AMA received $5 million from member dues and journal subscriptions and about half that from advertisements by drug companies, 10 years later, although its income from dues and subscriptions remained essentially the same, its income from the drug companies had quadrupled.

The AMA abandoned its watchdog role with respect to drugs, even opposing a bill proposed to require the pharmaceutical industry to demonstrate that their drugs were effective. Responding to public alarm over this issue, the Senate Subcommittee on Antitrust and Monopoly reported on how marketing efforts by drug companies had drastically altered what physicians and patients read about drugs. They found that ads in medical journals regularly gave biased assessments of drug benefits and risks. The committee was told of how medical journals declined to publish articles critical of drugs out of concern that revenues would suffer and of how drug companies gave financial incentives to influence magazine writers to publish positive articles about drugs in the press (Whitaker, 2002). The current highly extensive and sophisticated marketing practices of psychopharmacological drugs to psychiatrists, other doctors, and the general public dwarfs these earlier efforts and has led to an enormous expansion in the use of psychotropic drugs. Chapter 2 presents a more detailed analysis of how this has occurred and provides an assessment.

Questionable Claims in Biological Psychiatry

Psychiatry's promotion of psychotropic drugs to treat mental disorder is based upon a rationale that these drugs correct a chemical imbalance in the brain that is the cause of mental disorder. As we have indicated, frequently the analogy is made to the chemical imbalance in diabetes that is treated with insulin. The description provided earlier in this chapter regarding the research history that led to the understanding and treatment of diabetes makes clear that the use of insulin followed a series of objective findings having to do with a chemical imbalance that can be measured in the blood of diabetics. No such definitive findings or measurements exist of a chemical imbalance in the blood or brains of people with mental disorders when compared with normal people. Thus, in this analogy, a theory has been presented as if it is an established finding when it is not and does not fit the facts as we know them. Mental health practitioners, physicians, and the general public have been persuaded by a great deal of hype that something exists when there is, at least as yet, no good scientific basis for the claim.

Psychiatric drugs have come under increasing critical review by researchers. Significant problems have been cited in the research designs of many of the publications advancing the use of drugs. In addition, intrusive practices by the pharmaceutical industry have led to many questions about the validity of published research and the overutilization of drugs far beyond what has been tested in clinical trials. The issue of adverse drug side effects is only beginning to be properly recognized. Marketing practices and financial incentives provided by the pharmaceutical industry have led to concerns that there has been a loss in the integrity of the scientific literature on drugs and that researchers as well as regulators at the NIH and the Food and Drug Administration have been biased by payments from the drug companies. Chapter 2 addresses these issues.

Summary

Let's summarize what we have presented as the current state of affairs with respect to our understanding of mental disorder. First, we know that the advances in treatment of physical disorder came about as a result of application of the scientific method. Experiments and studies led to an understanding of basic processes and mechanisms of the body. This led to acceptance of the medical model and guided far more successful treatment of diseases understood in terms of these basic mechanisms. We also know that, while this medical model has been applied to explaining mental disorder, this has occurred in the absence of a similar understanding of the brain that would specify comparable mechanisms that account for disorders. For this reason, the theory is devoid of the underpinning that gives the medical model, when applied to physical disease, its validity.

Second, there is the question of what is meant by mental disorder and what is its etiology. Leaving aside what was defined as mental disorder in bygone times when we didn't know any better, in the present day we have a system for defining mental disorder (the DSM) that fails to meet the most basic criteria for acceptability. In the discussion of the DSM, we made the point that a system with low reliability cannot have much validity. The reverse, however, is also not true. High reliability in itself does not confer validity. In our review of the history of approaches to physical and mental disorder, there was high agreement (a definition of reliability) by the authorities of the day about theories that we now know to be bogus. Despite good reliability, once again there was poor validity. Thus, the fact that there is widespread agreement today by experts and the public on a biological theory to characterize mental disorder and explain its origin does not automatically impart validity to these ideas. Validity has to be established substantively.

Third, biological treatments in vogue today are the product of one branch of science, but there are other scientific investigations with a substantial base that argue against purely biological explanations. How biological factors are related to mental disorder remains unknown. Finally, the marketing of psychotropic medications as the first and only "proven" treatments for mental disorder is unsupported by research and is a product of economic rather than scientific forces. There are other treatment modalities that have as much or more backing, having arisen out of a very different theoretical orientation—one that places far more emphasis on experiences and learning. All of these issues are dealt with in more detail in subsequent chapters.

CHAPTER 2

WELCOME TO THE BRAVE NEW WORLD

This chapter covers the history of the current emphasis on psychopharmacology in psychiatry and examines how an aggressive marketing strategy of pharmaceutical companies has led to the current view of depression as an "illness" best treated by antidepressant medications. We also describe how the drug companies have created a mythology that implies that antidepressant medications are far more effective than they are.

While we want to make clear that it is a mistake to reduce human problems to biological illness, we believe that most psychiatrists wish to improve the lives of those who seek their help. However, it is evident that psychiatry has a strong incentive to believe in the disease model and in the efficacy of drugs. The pharmaceutical industry, like all corporations, has capital as its bottom line with the need for executives to report profits to investors. Not only do we maintain that the disease model has created confusion by accounting for human distress as "medical illness," the increasingly corporate structure of the health care system, including pharmaceutical and managed care companies, has often favored profit over people.

Marcia Angell, who was for twenty years editor of the highly regarded *New England Journal of Medicine,* has written a very informative book about the profiteering of the drug companies. Dubious marketing practices have made the pharmaceutical industry the most profitable industry in the United States, with Americans spending 200 billion dollars a year on prescription drugs. In 2001, while the median net return for all other industries was a little more than 3 percent of sales, it was more than 18 percent for the drug companies. Dr. Angell points out that the combined profits of the 10 drug companies listed in the Fortune 500 was more than the cumulative profits of the other 490 companies listed. She describes how new drugs are marketed as better and safer than older drugs, even when they are not, because this enables the industry to charge excessively for newer ("me-too") products. Although drug companies justify their pricing of drugs with the high cost of discovering and developing new drugs, Angell points out that these companies spend more on marketing and administration than on research and development. In 2000 the pharmaceutical industry spent 14 percent of sales on research and development and 31 percent on marketing and administration; that is, almost two-and-a-half times what it spent on research and development (Angell, 2004, 48).

The crisis for the field of psychiatry, which culminated in the early 1980s, as outlined in Chapter 1, has been resolved by the widespread public acceptance of prescribing psychopharmacological medications. As psychiatry has emphasized biological and biochemical treatments in a legitimate pursuit of treatments for human suffering, it has also gained its place as a more respected medical profession alongside physical medicine. However, as outlined in Chapter 1, it is important to recognize that the medical model upon which drug treatment rests lacks the definitive scientific underpinning that is present in other medical specialties, and therefore there is ample reason to question its validity. This model is one of several possible models for accounting for human disorder and has for many years been questioned from within the field psychiatry (for example, Szasz, 1974) and without (Pittu, 2002).

Biological Explanations for Behavioral Problems Are Appealing

Many people prefer viewing mental problems as physical in origin and therefore requiring physical treatments. Our culture still attaches some stigma to emotional problems, often making it an uncomfortable experience to speak about one's problems. Many people value their privacy and dislike the idea of talking openly about issues they find embarrassing. Moreover, behavioral change is hard work and psycho-therapy rarely progresses in a straight line. The prospect of a pill that would replace such a process can be very appealing.

We live in a culture of blame (Martell, Addis, & Jacobson, 2001). If someone experiences difficulty based on the culmination of life choices and environmental factors, he or she is easily judged as being either a failure or getting what he or she "deserves." Nobody wants that kind of blame thrust upon them. This mistaken notion that people should be blamed for their problems unless there is proof—usually in the form of a biological explanation that they can't help—has contributed importantly to the popularity of psychopharmacology. This kind of thinking also can be seen in the popularity of genetic explanations for many behaviors, particularly behaviors that are viewed by the majority of the public as deviant.

Take as an example a complex issue such as sexual orientation. Although there is much research to show that human beings (and other animals) have the capacity for wide variations in sexual behavior, and it is understood by all of the social scientific disciplines that sexual orientation is determined by multiple factors by the time an individual has reached late childhood or early adolescence (see for example, APA, 2000), reports of "gay genes" create a media stir. The thinking goes something like this: if sexual orientation is not determined by biology, then it is a choice. If sexual orientation is a choice, then those who "choose" to be gay are morally corrupt, whereas if there is a genetic or biological determination they are not culpable.

This thinking is flawed on a number of levels. First, biological determinism is not the only, nor is it a sufficient, explanation for the determinants of complex human behaviors. Many factors come into play—including evolutionary, biological/hormonal, and environmental components—to account for complex human experiences. Second, even behaviors that are nearly 100 percent environmentally determined do not necessarily allow for choice. For example, trauma is an environmental event, and many people who have experienced a traumatic event have recurrent nightmares, flashbacks, and so on later in life. One cannot say that they choose to have a flashback. Furthermore, even if the repeated re-experience of trauma alters brain chemistry in some way, this does not mean that biochemistry is the cause of the nightmares or flashbacks. Finally, we choose many things as human beings, from whether we will eat meat or only vegetarian food, to the type of religious affiliations we will have. In free societies, people can do so at will. There is no "culpability" for the choice of being a carnivore rather than a vegetarian. It is considered a free choice.

There are many examples of the appeal of biological explanations that account for behaviors as either outside the person's control because of genetic factors or represent examples of deviant, blame-worthy choices that people have made in their lives. Chromosomal abnormalities are sometimes blamed for the cause of certain men's extremely violent crimes, even though it is more likely that abnormal chromosomes may account for a propensity to aggression, but many other factors need to be present to create a murderer or rapist out of someone with a propensity to be aggressive. Men are expected to have an evolutionary push to mate with as many females as possible, while women are expected to have a need to find someone with whom they can form a lasting bond and raise children; thus, male philandering and female homemaking can be given a biological basis, despite the fact that male and female roles differ widely across cultures and gen-erations. These are but a few examples of how biology has provided a seemingly rational explanation for behavior that is of dubious explan-atory value. Such reasoning may appear plausible, even compelling, but it is far from complete.

Furthermore, many human problems are not easily solved. The experience of many people is that their depression or anxiety is extremely painful, seemingly recalcitrant, and feels like it is innate. Similarly, clinicians from all of the mental health professions recognize the frustration of seeing their clients suffer despite their best efforts to utilize well-established techniques and skill. Discoveries of therapeutic techniques and medical interventions that can relieve suffering are wel-comed by clients and clinicians alike. This is understandable. The prob-lem arises, however, when explanations become reductionistic and present as fact theories or findings that have not been firmly estab-lished by science.

A far better approach to understanding human behavior can be found in a biopsychosocial theory that recognizes biological, behavioral, and environmental influences in determining human behavior. Genetic and biological influences may play some role in problems such as depres-sion by setting varying thresholds of reactivity, but life experiences and the learning that has taken place in a context of responding to life's demands show the greatest influence on depression (Antonuccio, Danton, & DeNelsky, 1995). In other words, some people may indeed inherit a susceptibility to develop certain problems, but without an interaction of life experience and environmental factors such a predis-position would be unlikely to affect them. Moreover, it is very difficult to determine what is inherited and what is learned. Just because depres-sion may have been diagnosed in family members going back several generations, all we can know is that behavioral patterns, life philosophies, and DNA have been passed down. To say that any one of these factors trumps all of the other contributions is hopelessly reductionistic.

In the 1790s, it was believed that madness was caused by irregular actions of the blood vessels of the brain as a result of an injury to the brain, too much labor, extreme weather, constipation, masturbation, too much study, too much imagination, and so on (Whitaker, 2002). In 1796, Phillipe Pinell in France and the English Quakers began to use Moral Therapy to treat the "insane." Pinell rejected the former physiological explanations for madness on medical grounds, whereas the Quakers rejected such explanations on religious grounds (Whitaker, 2002). Whitaker notes that by 1874 state mental hospitals were becoming overcrowded, but legislators decided rather than provide humanitarian, caring staff to provide Moral Therapy, which was being shown at the time to be more effective, they would hire superintendents who disparaged this type of therapy as too costly. The focus was on managing budgets rather than treating people properly.

The situation in 1874 was not so different than the current situation in the twenty-first century when managed care companies try to cut care or push medication as the least expensive alternative. It is not uncommon for clinicians, highly trained in psychotherapy, who have collaborated with a client to work out a treatment plan that has led to slow and steady progress, to be told by managed care companies that they must send the client for a medication evaluation prior to having future sessions approved for reimbursement. Likewise, psychiatrists and psychiatric nurse practitioners who engage their clients in a psychotherapeutic process are often discouraged from doing this either by pressure from managed care companies to conduct only medication management or from the strong incentive of earning a better living by seeing more patients for shorter medication visits than lengthy psychotherapy. While managed care has rightly challenged the mental health profession to demonstrate proof of effectiveness, it has also brought the philosophy of corporate America to the health care system. The corporate profit motive and motivation to help those in need are usually contradictory values. Clinicians in all specialties are caught between the horns of a dilemma when they necessarily sign contracts with managed care companies in order to be reimbursed for their work but are, in effect, signing away much of the decision-making process regarding their clients' care to a distant third party.

Interestingly, although during the late twentieth century and into the beginning of the twenty-first century people have tended to have more empathy for those who have a biologically or genetically induced problem, the exact opposite was true in America in earlier times. In 1893, the American Medico-Psychological Association defined insanity as a symptom of bodily disease. When the American Eugenics Society was founded in 1922, its aim was to sterilize the lower classes, the mentally ill, the developmentally delayed, and some racial groups deemed "defective" to purify the gene pool. Blame was placed then on the "defective," and attempts were made to eliminate them. It is a sad fact that five early presidents of the American Psychological Association were members of the American Eugenics Society (Whitaker, 2002, p. 54). While there is no longer an American Eugenics Society, after such notions were taken to their horrifying conclusions in the Nazi death camps, the search for biological explanations of human suffering continues to this day. There is less likelihood today, however, of blaming the victim of a medical illness than there is of blaming someone who is struggling with the problems of living due to multiple factors of environment, biology, and learning history.

The Diabetes Metaphor

In Chapter 1, we looked at how diabetes often is used as a metaphor for the "disease" of mental disorder. Depressed patients are told that, "Just like diabetics need to take insulin, people who 'have depression' need to take medication." But, as we discussed earlier, there is no comparable imbalance in the blood of depressed patients and, as discussed in later chapters, depression is not something that one "has." Depression is more accurately conceptualized as a mood state with biological, cognitive, and behavioral manifestations, not a disease. However, if we consider the diabetes metaphor and look at the reality of the illness of diabetes, while there is a small minority of people who have early-onset diabetes treated only with insulin, the vast majority of people who develop diabetes do so not solely because of genetic or biological factors, but also as a result of a poor diet, improper exercise, and obesity. In fact, diabetes is often controllable through diet and exercise. Thus, the diabetes metaphor that we reject as an example of a biological cause for depression, in this sense becomes an apt metaphor for depression.

A more apt analogy for depression would be allergies and allergic reactions. Some individuals are born with certain vulnerabilities to environmental stimuli that cause a reaction. Others become sensitized to certain allergens over a lifespan, and develop allergies later in life.

Without the environmental exposure, however, the person would not have an allergic reaction. For those that become depressed the same may very well hold true. Some people may be born with or develop the vulnerability to experience negative life events in a way that makes them more anxious and depressed. When childhood environments provide toxic rather than ameliorative experiences, depression becomes potentially chronic with all of the psychological, biological, and behavioral systems maintaining it. Others become sensitized over a longer period of time, through lifetimes of disappointment, loss, or bombardment with adversity. Without the interaction of the person and the environment, however, there is no "disease" entity waiting to pounce. However, just like allergies, depression can cause great suffering and needs to be addressed appropriately to improve the person's life.

Depression is the result of many variables, including perhaps certain predispositions to blue moods or melancholy, early environment, learning history and development, and ongoing cognitive and behavioral patterns that exacerbate and eventually create the problem. There is considerable reason to understand depression as a response to difficulties in life prompted by avoidance behaviors that interfere with people making use of their abilities to accomplish goals that are important to them. Much more is said about this formulation in later chapters, but just as in the case of diabetes, where the problem is often controlled with diet and exercise without medication, depression is most often best treated by promoting targeted changes in behavior.

It is likely that biological phenomena associated with psychological functioning will continue to be discovered. This should not shock us, but we do need to be careful what we make of it. Scientists no longer believe in dualistic separations of mind and body. Changes occur in the brain as we move our muscles, integrate new information from the environment, or feel emotions. Evidence has disclosed that sometimes these changes in the brain precede behavior and sometimes they follow behavior. Even if problems can be attributed to biology, biological treatments are not necessarily the best treatments. We have noted this in the example of diabetes. It is also true of musculoskeletal problems. After physical injuries that tear muscles, long-term treatment with muscle relaxants and painkillers is typically discouraged, and physical therapy is the treatment of choice. Not only does physical therapy have fewer negative side effects like addiction or cognitive confusion, it also provides more permanent results. The same is true regarding emotional problems. Medications are one option, but as we will discuss later, outcomes are shorter lived than those found with cognitive behavioral therapies, and there are significant adverse side effects associated with medications.

The Medical Model Applied to Behavioral Disorders

Many biological therapies have been discovered by accident. Sometimes an explanation or theory of the cause of the disorder follows. This is typified in the field of psychiatry, where so little is known about brain chemistry and where there is a strong desire to offer a biological explanation for mental disorder. The interested reader is referred to Valenstein (1998) for a comprehensive review and critique of the various drugs that were discovered accidentally in pursuit of treatments for other purposes that then were noticed to have properties that could be applied to explaining and treating mental disorders. For example, chlorpromazine, a drug often used in treating psychoses, was discovered while studying synthetic dyes important to the coal-tar industry. It was noticed that the substances being studied had sedative and euphoric effects. Tranquilizers that are prevalent in the treatment of anxiety conditions arose in the course of studying gram-negative microorganisms; it was noticed that they produced a kind of muscular paralysis, which was called "tranquilization," before it was thought to apply them to anxiety conditions. Antidepressant drugs originated from the study of V-2 rocket fuel in World War II. Substances studied in rocket fuel research were found to have some usefulness in the treatment of tuberculosis. It then was observed that tubercular patients who were administered the drug showed signs of euphoria, leading to the idea of using the drug to treat depression.

There is nothing inherently wrong about discovering treatments in this way, but one must be cautious about their interpretation. More often than not, claims made on this basis turn out to be false because the reasoning is backward, and it has no experimental foundation. Unlike findings that come about as extensions of a line of systematic research, accidental discoveries have no guiding context. As a result, what is made of them is speculative, based upon assumptions about their basic mechanism, which may or may not be true. It is only through further research of the noticed effect that the "discovery" can be put into some understandable perspective. What we make of the effect we have noticed requires corroboration. In the case of psychiatric drugs, including the antidepressants that are the prime subject of this book, these accidental findings have often led to wide acceptance of the drug before their usefulness and safety have been satisfactorily confirmed.

What follows is a brief description—based on Valenstein's (1998) comprehensive study—of the psychiatric drug therapies that have been espoused and prescribed over time. In each case, the treatment arose because of an effect that was noticed in studying drugs of interest for some other purpose. This effect was then deemed to be of value for treating some emotional disorder. In the 1920s, sleep therapy was the treatment of choice made possible by administering barbiturates that caused patients to sleep for long periods. Convulsive therapy was used in the 1930s, with the convulsions being induced by drugs like Metrazol and insulin. Neither of these approaches is viewed any longer to have value or to be safe. The 1950s saw the advent of the "miracle drugs" that have to this day continued to be developed, greatly profiting the pharmaceutical companies by offering quick fixes to life's problems. Chlorpromazine (brand name Thorazine) was introduced in 1955. Over two million prescriptions had been written for Thorazine even before the National Institute of Mental Health had conducted a placebo controlled trial of the drug. Once widespread in its use for a number of psychiatric diagnoses, chlorpromazine now is restricted to use as an antipsychotic medication because of the serious deleterious side effects that slowly came to light. Another antipsychotic medication, Haloperidol, was introduced in 1957. This drug also was considered to be miraculous until it, too, was discovered to have serious side effects that developed with prolonged use. Its acceptability is now greatly curtailed.

The first antidepressant medications were introduced in 1952. These were the monoamine oxidase inhibitors, which produced dangerous side effects if patients ate certain foods that were rich in tyramine. During this same period, the tricyclic antidepressants were discovered. Lithium was being used in the 1940s to treat mania, although it was not approved by the FDA until 1970. Antianxiety agents, the benzodiazepines like Valium, were also developed in the 1960s and by 1975 over 100 million prescriptions had been filled.

These drugs had moderate effects on people suffering from depression or severe anxiety, but they were addictive and their use did not develop from a coherent understanding of the etiology of the problems. In the case of all of these drugs the reasoning is backward. When the drugs are developed, the biochemical processes that they affect are considered to be the cause of psychological problems.

For example, in 1962, Stein speculated that depression may arise from a deficiency in the reward system in the brain since many people become depressed even when the environment "supplies a normal amount of rewarding stimulation" (Valenstein, 1998, p. 66). This starts as a testable theory from observation of depressed patients. However, because antidepressant medications seemed to have positive effects for some people, and because it was known that the neurotransmitter system (the chemicals that are emitted between nerves in the brain as a method of "communication") had an effect on the experience of reward, it was then argued that depression was caused by an "imbalance" of the brain's neurotransmitters. This hypothesis seemingly was supported by the finding that the neurotransmitters norepinephrine, serotonin, and dopamine are all decreased by the drug reserpine, which was used in the 1950s and 1960s to treat schizophrenia and anxiety. Because reserpine decreased these three neurotransmitters and caused sedation and lethargy in patients, it was hypothesized that depression was caused by low levels of these neurotransmitters. Some theorists believed norepinephrine was most closely associated with depression, while others thought serotonin was most important. However, it was later discovered that reserpine does not precipitate clinical depression, although it may exacerbate symptoms in those already predisposed to depression. Despite the popularity of the theory that depression is caused by chemical imbalances, there is no definitive support for this conclusion (Akiskal, 1995; Valenstein, 1998).

> Biochemical theories of mental disorders are at present floundering although only a few are willing to admit it. The initial biochemical theories are clearly inadequate to explain either drug action or the etiology of mental illness, but it is not known what can replace them.... While it might be assumed that all the additional knowledge of brain chemistry would make it easier to understand how psychotherapeutic drugs work and what causes mental disorders, in actuality it has just multiplied the number of interacting variables that must be considered. (Valenstein, 1998, p.124)

The 10–20–30 Year Pattern

Joseph Glenmullen, a Harvard psychiatrist, has described what he calls the 10–20–30 Year Pattern of psychiatric drug usage, which begins with the discovery of a new drug that is highly touted and aggressively marketed as a miraculous breakthrough far superior to its predecessors. In the beginning, a few doctors are ardent advocates, sometimes aided by celebrities endorsing the drugs as having been amazingly helpful. General practitioners then begin prescribing the drug to large numbers of people for more and more conditions. It takes about 10 years for development of recognition that there are problems with these drugs, during which period they are heavily defended by the drug companies and physicians advocating the drugs. After about 20 years, enough data have accumulated that doubts begin to take hold, and it takes another 10 years before the drug is abandoned in favor of a new miracle drug. He describes this pattern as a historical one that has unfolded in the prescribing of cocaine, amphetamines, barbiturates, tranquilizers, the tricyclics, and now has begun to play out with the selective serotonin reuptake inhibitors (SSRIs) of Prozac, Zoloft, Paxil, and Luvox.

The human brain has incredible plasticity. Experience can change brain anatomy (Greenaugh, Black, & Wallace, 1987). We are not arguing that changes in the brain do not occur, or that they are not associated with moods and other psychological processes. Indeed, studies of cerebral blood flow (CBF) have found that there are changes in the amount of CBF in different parts of the brain under certain conditions. Changes in CBF have been found to result from meditative prayer (Newberg, Pourdehnad, M., Alavi, A., & d'Aquili, E.G. 2003), hypnosis (Rainville et al., 1999), and cognitive-behavioral therapy (Furmark et al., 2002). The point is that brain chemistry is associated with all human behavior. However, these interactions are complex and cannot be reduced in simple cause-effect fashions. For example, it may be true that people who are depressed show differences in cerebral blood flow. However, knowing this does not suggest that overactivity or deficiencies in one part of the brain predated depression and therefore caused it. It is equally possible that poor diet, inactivity, brooding over life problems, and many other common symptoms of depression, over long periods of time, can change processes in the brain. Medication, psychotherapy, meditation, and, most likely, taking a brisk walk and noticing the beauty of one's surroundings, can all have an impact on the biological structures of the brain. To say that depression, social anxiety, and fears of snakes or slithering objects (that is, certain types of phobias) are illnesses is to use a metaphor that is of very little value in finding appropriate methodologies for improving a person's well-being. The metaphor may even motivate people to accept, uncritically, the claims of proponents of medications and limit their choices to purely pharmacological treatments for these so-called illnesses.

Just How Effective Are Antidepressant Medications?

The National Institute of Mental Health funded a major study to assess the efficacy of antidepressant medications, psychotherapy, or a combination treatment compared to a placebo (Elkin et al., 1989). The study demonstrated that active medication was effective in treating severe depression, but medication did not have any advantage over pill-placebo for less severely depressed patients. Nevertheless, the Agency for Health Care Policy and Research (AHCPR) published a set of clinical practice guidelines for treatment of depression in primary care settings that favored pharmacotherapy as the first choice treatment rather than psychotherapy (Depression Guideline Panel, 1993). Such recommendations encourage primary care physicians to prescribe antidepressant medications for their patients who are mildly depressed, despite the fact that there is little or no evidence to support such a prescription practice. These recommendations also suggested that psychotherapy should be tried only after attempts with three medications failed.

Follow-up data from the NIMH collaborative study showed that the psychotherapies outperformed the drug on nearly every measure at 18-month follow-up (Shea et al., 1992). Yet the AHCPR recommended medication first, despite the additional finding that relapse is more likely following medication than psychotherapy.

Several investigators have questioned this enthusiasm about the effectiveness of antidepressant medications. In 1998, Kirsch and Saperstein conducted a meta-analysis of 20 studies comparing antidepressant medications to pill-placebo representing data on 2,328 patients. Meta-analysis is a mathematical technique for comparing the data from multiple studies that meet certain selection criteria, allowing the investigators to make rational comparisons between studies that are similar in design. Based on their analyses, they concluded that 75 percent of the effect of antidepressant medications is accounted for by the placebo effect that accompanies taking medication. In a more recent meta-analysis, Kirsch, Moore, Scoboria, and Nicholls (2002) re-analyzed the efficacy data reported to the Food and Drug Administration (FDA) for approval of six widely prescribed antidepressant medications: Prozac, Paxil, Zoloft, Effexor, Serzone, and Celexa. The analysis included 47 randomized placebo controlled trials for the six drugs. A randomized placebo controlled trial assigns patients to drug or placebo conditions at random and uses double-blind procedures whereby supposedly neither the patient nor the prescriber knows whether the patient is on the active drug or the placebo. Kirsch, Moore, Scoboria, and Nicholls analyzed the differences as reported by means of a commonly used physician administered assessment for depression (the Hamilton Depression Scale). In efficacy studies, the average change on the scale was about two points, which was not clinically significant. The authors concluded that 82 percent of the drug response was due to placebo effects. While the authors concluded that about 18 percent of the drug response was due to the pharmacological agent in the medication, even this small number is open to question given the intrusiveness of the drug companies in this research. Valenstein (1998) and others we will cite later in this chapter have described how the drug industry influences what research is done, what is and is not reported, sampling problems, and the selectivity that occurs in determining which investigators are supported. Consequently, it is reasonable to question how much of this remaining 18 percent is due to artifacts attributable to bias.

In fact, Moore, who was one of the authors of this analysis, has since provided additional information on the study he did with Kirsch. He states that it is likely that the drug effect of 18 percent is an inflated figure because investigators did not have access to unpublished studies from FDA files that failed to show any drug effect. When he and Kirsch included these 40 studies, the difference between drugs and placebos was even smaller. For Prozac, the placebo accounted for 89 percent of the antidepressant effect. Looking at 1,500 patients in five studies, the Prozac patients improved about eight points compared with seven points for those on placebo (Moore, 1999).

Fisher and Greenberg (1989) in their review of the antidepressant effects of the tricyclic compounds and monoamine oxidase inhibitors, found rampant problems in the design of these studies. After reviewing a large number of studies, they conclude there is a 15 percent improvement advantage of these antidepressant drugs over placebo, a figure not far from that cited by Kirsch (2002) and his colleagues for the SSRIs.

Outcomes of placebo-controlled clinical trials are further complicated by the fact that the "blind" in double-blind studies often is broken by either the patient or the physician (Antonuccio, Danton, & DeNelsky, 1995). The presence or absence of side effects may influence a patient's or rater's perceptions, providing another kind of placebo effect. Patients who recognize they are on a placebo may expect less in the way of results. The "placebo effects" of the medication as they ordinarily are understood no longer apply. Alternatively, patients who experience side effects, knowing they are taking active medication, may respond because the knowledge that they are on a real medication serves as a placebo. Physicians, because of the reported side effects, also often can differentiate between patients on an active drug or a placebo, and this knowledge can affect the objectivity of their clinical ratings. This breaking of the blind is particularly likely in studies that use inert placebos such as sugar pills rather than an active placebo that provides no antidepressant effect, but mimics the side effects of the active medication. Unfortunately, only a handful of studies have made use of active placebos. Fisher and Greenberg's review found that in studies that made use of active placebos, whatever superiority had been reported for the drug over the placebo vanished.

Why Have So Many Chosen to Take Antidepressants?

Figures released in December 2004 by the Centers for Disease Control of the federal government indicate that the use of antidepressant medications has almost tripled in the last decade and that 1 in 10 American women now take antidepressant medication. During the year 2002, women visiting their physician's office were prescribed a psychotropic medication in one out of three of those visits (Vedantam, 2004a).

A very important question about the widespread use of antidepressants is why they are so popular, given the body of scientific evidence that shows that the effect of these drugs can barely be distinguished from the effects of taking a placebo (Moore, 1999). The primary answer to this question is to be found in the enormous amount of money the pharmaceutical industry spends on advertising and the expertise they have demonstrated in how they spend this money. Drug companies spend $100 million a day on advertising (Wolfe, 2003). Just as advertising has created a great demand for many products, it has achieved a similar effect in promoting a desire for psychiatric drugs by persuading people that these drugs are the best means of relieving their suffering. Here are some of the ways this has been done:

1. Sales Efforts Made Directly to MDs. Since antidepressants are prescription drugs, their sale is dependent upon doctors prescribing them, just as is the case with other prescription drugs. Consequently, the drug companies have targeted enhancing the writing of these prescriptions in a number of ways.

The drug companies employ 87,000 sales representatives who visit doctors' offices to sell doctors on the virtues of their products, backed up with favorable literature selected by the drug companies. Moore (1999) did some checking on this literature by looking into what is printed with the packaging of the antidepressant Serzone, which is touted as having significantly helped two-thirds of patients. He discovered that the insert that accompanied the drug declared the drug to have been proven superior over placebo in two clinical trials. However, when he looked into this claim, he found that Bristol-Myers had done eight studies of Serzone, not two. In the six studies that were not mentioned, the drug had no measurable effect. In addition, in one of the two studies cited, the drug effect was found only after some of the patients who improved on the placebo or did poorly on the drug were dropped from the study.

The pharmaceutical industry spends almost six billion dollars a year on direct marketing to physicians. In all likelihood many doctors are not recipients of this largesse. Nevertheless, on a per capita basis this works out to $6,000–$7,000 per doctor. This money is for meals, travel, parties, and gift certificates. Merck was so pleased with one doctor's prescribing of Vioxx that a company representative gave him a gift of season tickets to the Philadelphia Eagles (Cha, 2005). Stephen Cha, an internist at Yale, points out that such perks raise questions about how much this influences the prescribing practices of doctors. Dr. Sidney Wolfe, Editor of the Public Citizen Research Group, also reported in testimony he gave to Congress in 2003 that Wyeth was giving doctors 1,000 frequent flyer points in return for each new patient prescribed a particular heart medication, and Roche was paying doctors $1,700 when they prescribed their antibiotic. He cited another drug company, TAP, which was found to have illegally induced doctors to prescribe overpriced medication costing the U.S. government hundreds of millions of dollars. TAP agreed to pay $1.5 billion in criminal and civil damages for health care fraud that "dwarfs anything seen in the recent round of Wall Street's merchant bank settlements" (Wolfe, 2003).

2. Continuing Medical Education. Through offering continuing medical education, which states require of doctors to maintain their licenses, drug companies hire experts who will promote their drugs by presenting favorable data about their products. As an enticement to enroll, these tax-deductible seminars are generally held at beautiful resorts or in attractive cities with plenty of free time and gifts. Wolfe (2003) and Duncan, Miller, and Sparks (2000) have cited studies of how effective these presentations are in influencing the prescribing behaviors of the attending doctors. In one study, 17 of the 20 doctors were certain prior to the experience that they would not be influenced

by such medical education in any significant way. However, their pre-scribing habits changed dramatically—tenfold in one case, fourfold in another—after having been "educated" in these drug company–spon-sored seminars.

3. Funding of Research. Drug companies fund research that has been designed and presented in publications in ways that give a favorable impression of their drugs. The curtailment in federal funding of grants that began during Reagan's presidency has led to drug companies funding the majority of clinical trials of drugs. Of the 315 published clinical trials of 29 antidepressant drugs that have been identified, all of the named sponsors were drug companies (Duncan, Miller, & Sparks, 2000). Funding by companies that have an important stake in the outcome of research has had its consequences. An example is found in a very influential article in the *Journal of the American Medical Association* concerning Celebrex, an anti-arthritis drug with blockbuster sales (Wolfe, 2003). (A blockbuster drug is defined as a drug with sales of over a billion dollars per year.) Wolfe reports that this article, which testified to the advantages of Celebrex (including its having fewer side effects of ulcers compared to other drugs), was later discovered to have been funded by Pfizer, the manufacturer of Celebrex, and the authors of the study were all paid by Pfizer. Furthermore, the study reported results for only the first six months, not the full results that were available to the researchers. When the full results were analyzed independently, it was found that Celebrex, in addition to being far more expensive than the older drugs, had other potentially harmful cardiac side effects. Another article (Stelfox, Chua, O'Rourke, & Detsky, 1998) reported on researchers who had published studies on the use of calcium channel blockers to treat high blood pressure and angina. Ninety-six percent of the articles written in support of these drugs were written by researchers who had financial connections to the drug companies, whereas only 37 percent of researchers who published articles that did not support the drugs had any relationship with drug companies. Wolfe deplores a "systematic bias" in medical research sponsored by the pharmaceutical companies. He quotes Dr. Arnold Reiman, a Harvard professor and a former editor of the prestigious *New England Journal of Medicine*: "The medical profession is being bought by the pharmaceutical industry, not only in terms of the prac-tice of medicine, but also in terms of teaching and research.... I think it is a disgrace" (Wolfe, 2003).

Richard Smith, editor of the *British Medical Journal*, has written a strong warning about how the pharmaceutical industry is manipulating the results of drug studies to make their products appear better than they are. He cites Richard Horton, editor of *Lancet*, another highly respected medical journal, who wrote, "Journals have devolved into information laundering operations for the pharmaceutical industry," (quoted in Smith, 2005) and Jerry Kassirer, a former editor of *The New England Journal of Medicine*, who wrote that the pharmaceutical industry has "deflected the moral compasses of many physicians" (quoted in Smith, 2005). Smith states that while journals are dependent on advertising income from the pharmaceutical industry and accept ads that may often be misleading, the larger problem has to do with the publication of clinical trials conducted by the industry that carry the journal's stamp of approval (unlike advertising) and which are highly influential with doctors who receive reprints of these articles. In 1994 a study was conducted of all trials funded by manufacturers of nonsteroidal anti-inflammatory drugs for arthritis. All 56 studies showed results favorable to the company. In every case the new drug was found to be as good or better than the competitor's product. In 2003 a study was done to compare 30 drug outcome studies funded by the pharmaceutical industry versus studies funded by other sources. Studies funded by the industry were found to be four times more likely to show results favorable to the company than studies funded by other sources. Smith states that it took him almost 25 years as an editor to catch on to what was happening. Because the studies were well-designed they were favorably reviewed for publication and became highly influential. He determined that the pharmaceutical industry gets the results they want not by tampering with the results, but by asking the "right" questions. They then engage in various publishing strategies to gain maximum exposure of the positive results. He gives examples of methods used, such as: conduct a trial of your drug against a treatment known to be inferior, trial your drug against too low a dose of a competitor's drug, conduct a trial of your drug against too high a dose of a competitor's drug (making your drug less toxic), conduct trials that are too small to show differences from another drug, or use multiple endpoints in the trial and select for publication those that give favorable results.

While these examples are not of antidepressant drugs, is there not reason from such examples to suspect that there could be similar problems with respect to antidepressants that also have blockbuster sales?

4. The National Institutes of Health. Drug companies have engaged in questionable acts by hiring researchers and evaluators of research at the National Institutes of Health (NIH). Following a series of articles in the *Los Angeles Times* (Willman, 2003) and a subsequent swelling of public

concern, congressional hearings were held in 2004 regarding the number of scientists at the NIH who were on retainer and had other financial connections to drug companies. Investigators found more than 100 cases of scientists who had not reported income, as required by NIH regulations, who were receiving money from drug companies, including payments by means of stock options. In one case, Pfizer had paid a researcher more than half a million dollars in consulting fees, honoraria, and expense reimbursements. While these scientists protested the implication that they had been biased by their financial remuneration, there is reason to be concerned about such an effect.

5. The Food and Drug Administration. The Food and Drug Administration, which is allegedly the public's watchdog regarding the effectiveness and safety of drugs, has failed to exercise appropriate oversight of the pharmaceutical industry, allowing the business interests of the drug companies to take precedence over the health and safety interests of the public. Sommers-Flanagan (1996) reviewed the literature on tricyclic antidepressants and SSRIs in the treatment of depressed youth. They concluded that neither of these medications demonstrated greater efficacy than placebo in the treatment of depression for children and adolescents. Yet until recent alarming reports on the induction of suicidal behaviors by SSRIs, prompted by the urging of the drug industry, primary care doctors and pediatricians increasingly prescribed antidepressants to children and adolescents. Between 1988 and 1994, there was a three- to fivefold increase in antidepressant medication treatments for children ages 2 to 19. In 2003, British authorities, after reviewing the research, warned against this practice as leading to increased suicidal behavior in some of these children. The FDA refused to issue a similar warning even though its own in-house research conducted by its senior epidemiologist corroborated the British conclusion. Moreover, the FDA, maintaining its position that these drugs were valuable, repeatedly urged manufacturers of antidepressants not to disclose to physicians and the public that these drugs had been found no more effective than placebo and sometimes were found to incite dangerous behaviors. The FDA's own researcher, whose job is to assess the safety of medicines, upon reviewing 22 studies of antidepressants, found that nearly twice as many children on drugs became suicidal as those on placebo. Newman (2004) reported that suicide experts from Columbia University reviewed the narratives of adverse-event reports from the FDA and concluded that the rate of definite or possible suicidality among children and adolescents receiving antidepressants was twice the rate for those receiving placebo. Furthermore, Newman

reevaluated the Treatments for Adolescent Depression material (Silva, Petrycki, et al., 2004, as cited in Newman, 2004) and concluded that the benefits of fluoxetine over placebo was too small to outweigh the risk of increased suicidality (Newman, 2004). A similar story is found in the recent revelations about the arthritis drug Vioxx. The FDA's handling of Vioxx has received a good deal of attention and, because the story has features that parallel the FDA's handling of antidepressants with children, it is quite relevant. Nearly a year before Merck withdrew Vioxx from the market, it had results from studies of patient records that the drug posed cardiovascular risks. A top FDA reviewer, Dr. David Graham, reported that "agency higher-ups discounted his efforts to call attention to the drug's problems" (Meier, 2004). As a consequence of the disclosures about Vioxx, Senator Charles Grassley (R-Iowa), Chairman of the Senate Finance Committee, held hearings in November 2004 to investigate the FDA. Senator Grassley stated: "It's obvious that the leadership of the agency must take on what look like deep-rooted problems when it comes to putting public health and safety first and public relations second" (Harris, 2004d). The investigation revealed that in the past four years, the FDA's policing of harmful side effects has been markedly reduced. For example, between 1996 and 2001, 10 important drugs were removed from the market, compared with three between 2001 and 2004, and two of those three were removed in the early months of the Bush administration. The number of warning letters sent by the FDA's drug marketing office that challenged misleading or dishonest drug ads also declined sharply from 480 such cease-and-desist letters between 1996 and 2001 to 130 letters in the last four years. This is despite the fact that the number of reports of harmful side effects from approved drugs had almost doubled between 1996 and 2004 (Kaufman and Masters, 2004). Said Senator Grassley: "The kind of mismanagement we've seen this year by the Food and Drug Administration demands tough scrutiny. One of my concerns is that the FDA has a relationship with the drug companies that is too cozy." Some in Congress have been reported to be concerned as well by court cases in which the FDA intervened on the side of drug and medical device makers sued by patients who claimed they were harmed (Kaufman and Masters, 2004). Dr. Eric Topol, chairman of the department of cardiovascular medicine at the Cleveland Clinic studied Vioxx and wrote an op-ed piece in the *New York Times* about the failures of Merck and the FDA to accurately report on the dangers of this drug (Topol, 2004). Topol cites a 2001 study he and others published in the *Journal of the American Medical Association* demonstrating

the significant heart attack risk of Vioxx, which was not withdrawn
from the market because of this risk until 2004, three years later. Their
study had demonstrated that when compared to a commonly used over-
the-counter anti-inflammatory medication, Vioxx had a five times
greater heart attack risk. For years, Merck disputed these findings. He
deplores the FDA's absence of oversight. Making the identical point,
Sidney Wolfe's *Health Letter* issued warnings against the use of Vioxx
two years before the FDA acted to remove the drug from the market
(Wolfe, 2004). Merrill Goozner, director of the Integrity in Science
Project at the Center for Science in the Public Interest, recently wrote:

To make rational choices, doctors and consumers need the FDA and
other agencies to be independent arbiters of not just the safety and effi-
ciency of new drugs and devices, but of their relative medical usefulness
and economic viability. Moreover, the medical oversight system needs a
new ethic—one that scrupulously adheres to a standard that says its
studies and decisions have been made entirely free of commercial bias
and conflicts of interest. Sadly, that is very far from the situation today.
Drug and device companies sponsor most clinical trials; FDA advisory
panels are larded with scientists tied to private companies; corporate
user fees help finance the FDA that is conducting reviews; doctors get
most of their medical information either from sales representatives of
drug companies or corporate-sponsored continuing medical education;
and the companies are given primary responsibility for post-marketing
safety surveillance of their own products. (Goozner, 2004)

6. Direct-to-Consumers Advertising of Prescription Drugs. The pharmaceutical industry's lobbying efforts paid off in 1997, when the FDA
lifted its ban on direct advertising of prescription drugs to consumers.
Prescription drugs are now advertised directly to the public to create a
demand for these drugs by influencing doctors to prescribe them. In
2003 the pharmaceutical industry spent $3.2 billion on such advertis-
ing. Sales of the 50 most advertised drugs increased by 32 percent from
1999 to 2000, compared with 14 percent for all other drugs (Hollon,
2005). If you watch television, you can see the amount of money that is
put into marketing. There are advertisements for allergy medications,
arthritis medications, and antidepressants, as well as other products
that require a prescription from a doctor. Unfortunately, the advertisements do not always report the entire story. An ad for Paxil (paroxetine) claims that it is the "only proven treatment for social anxiety
disorder" and shows images of worried, shy people looking relaxed and
happy at parties. What the ad does not report is that behavior therapy
and cognitive-behavior therapy have not only been proven effective in

the treatment of social anxiety, they have consistently outperformed medication in clinical trials.

Antidepressant medications are among the most heavily advertised drugs to the public (Kravitz et al., 2005). The rationale that has been given for allowing this type of advertising (which is allowed only in the United States and New Zealand) is that it encourages patients to seek effective treatment that is available. The argument that has been raised against it is that it encourages overtreatment. Nearly 80 percent of physicians believe this type of advertising leads patients to request treatments they do not need. The recently reported problems associated with COX-2 inhibitors are illustrative. In the year 2000, these drugs were the most heavily advertised to consumers, exceeding the advertising for Pepsi and Budweiser. The quadrupled use of these drugs from 1999 to 2000 occurred primarily among patients with low risk of adverse reactions from the use of less expensive, nonsteroidal anti-inflammatory drugs (Hollon, 2005).

A recently published study with respect to anti-depressant medication focused on exploring the extent to which doctors are influenced in how they treat their patients because of direct to consumer advertising. Actors were trained to make visits to doctors' offices simulating two kinds of patients, one group presenting signs of major depression, the other signs of an adjustment disorder with depressed mood. These two groups were selected because the psychiatric literature supports the use of anti-depressant medication for the first group, but not the second. Within each group, some actors mentioned viewing a TV ad for anti-depressant medication and others did not. The study found that for physicians examining patients in the adjustment disorder group, when there was no statement about a TV ad for an anti-depressant, physicians were unlikely to prescribe an anti-depressant. Prescription rates increased significantly following mention of having viewed a TV ad for an anti-depressant along with raising a question as to whether the doctor thought it would help. The authors conclude that when a patient cites a TV ad for an anti-depressant, in the context of symptoms that do not warrant such a prescription, doctors are significantly more likely to offer care that is excessive. (Kravitz et al., 2005)

7. Consumer Advocacy Groups. A number of mental health consumer advocacy groups, all of which endorse a biological viewpoint in explaining psychiatric disorder, are heavily funded by drug companies. For example, the Anxiety Disorders Association of America, which has as its aim "the prevention and cure of anxiety disorders," has received 75 percent of its income from pharmaceutical companies;

the National Depressive and Manic Depressive Association, whose purpose is to provide education about "depressive and manic-depressive illness as medical diseases," has received 91 percent of its income from pharmaceutical companies; the National Mental Illness Screening Project, which sponsors such events as "National Depression Screening Day" in schools, received 48 percent of its income from Eli Lilly (Duncan, Miller, and Sparks, 2000). Thus, the nature of the advocacy offered by these groups appears to have been largely financed by the pharmaceutical industry.

8. The American Psychiatric Association. At least 30 percent of the budget of the American Psychiatric Association is paid for by the pharmaceutical companies by means of grants, advertisements in journals, and payments for exhibits at its meetings (Duncan et al., 2000).

Given the amount of money being spent with the degree of marketing sophistication the pharmaceutical industry possesses, is it any wonder that the overblown story of the effectiveness of antidepressant drugs has been successfully sold to practitioners and the general public?

Protecting the Integrity of Science

As some professional organizations have become more aware of the effects of these pharmaceutical industry practices, a number of institutions concerned with science have seen the need to protect the integrity of science from such incursions. Much of this concern has not yet translated into greater public understanding of the truth about some of these drugs. It is important for this to happen if the mythology about drugs is to be brought to an end.

The power of the pharmaceutical industry to influence what research is done, how it is reported, and to determine what is and is not reported is a problem of unprecedented proportions. There are reasons to be concerned that the bank of published research on which we depend for advancement of our scientific knowledge is being corrupted by the pharmaceutical industry's zeal for profit. This is a very serious issue for all of us, and efforts that are underway to rectify this problem are extremely important. Here are a number of actions that have been taken to protect the integrity of science:

1. By Scientific Journals. The editors of a number of scientific journals recently adopted rules requiring that authors of articles submitted for publication disclose their financial ties to the pharmaceutical industry. This information is published with the articles. As a result, readers are

in a position to assess the article in light of this connection. In addition, because of the drug industry's practice of only permitting publication of favorable articles, a number of journals have adopted a policy that before considering articles for publication, clinical trials must be registered in a public data base when they are initiated. By this means, reports of favorable results may be considered in context.

2. By the Government. Congressional hearings have been held, and, as noted above, some significant penalties have been exacted against drug companies for false claims as a deterrent to their illegal practices. The attorney general of New York, Eliot Spitzer, sued GlaxoSmithKline, resulting in a $2.5 million settlement of a suit that alleged the company had hidden results showing that Paxil may have been responsible for increased suicidal ideation in children and teenagers (Harris, 2004b). An agreement was reached with the pharmaceutical industry that companies would disclose the results of all clinical trials, rather than cherry-picking favorable results and hiding unfavorable ones. Eli Lilly has been faithful to the agreement, posting all of its clinical trials on a government Web site set up for this purpose. But Merck, Glaxo-SmithKline, and Pfizer have been evading the agreement by refusing to name the drugs they are testing. By not naming the drugs, it is difficult to determine how many times a drug has been tested (Berenson, 2005). As a result, a number of journals have announced they will refuse to publish results of clinical trials that violate the reporting standard. Federal legislation has been advocated for stiff penalties for noncompliance (Hiding data on drug trials, 2005).

Three years ago Vermont enacted a law with the intention of controlling the billions of dollars awarded by the pharmaceutical industry to individual doctors. The law requires that drug companies make public all promotional gifts and payments to doctors. Such laws are passed on the theory that sunshine will control ethically questionable practices. Unfortunately, patients in Vermont are no more aware of such payments than they were before the law was passed because the pharmaceutical companies have found ways to circumvent the new rules (Cha, 2005).

3. By the NIH. Following the congressional hearings, the NIH put a lid on the amount of money that government scientists may earn from drug companies whose products these scientists are studying or overseeing. Rules have been established that prohibit stock options as payment for outside consulting (Weiss, 2004). This has provided greater reassurance that decisions made at the NIH are based on scientific evidence and not because of inappropriate influences (Zerhouni, 2005).

4. By the FDA. It took about 10 years, but faced with rising public and professional opposition to their stance, and the report of a federal advisory panel that antidepressants appeared to lead some children to become suicidal, the FDA finally reversed its stance. Agency officials now state that studies have shown that an increase in suicidal tendencies in children is not the result of the children's underlying depression, but was caused by the medications (Harris, 2004b, 2004c; Vedantam, 2004c).

The ubiquity of physical and emotional suffering ensures that purveyors of treatments of dubious value will always be with us. When it comes to physical illness, our considerable understanding of the basis for disorder gives reason to have confidence that most of the drugs commonly in use have value and are safe. The same assertion cannot be made with respect to psychiatric drugs for which this basic underlying understanding is missing. We believe that drug companies prefer to sell the real thing. However, the record, unfortunately, is clear that these companies, if allowed to do so, will continue to sell highly profitable drugs despite knowledge of evidence of harmful side effects.

Some Caution, Nonetheless

Having written all of this, it is possible that evaluating large-scale trials and averaging data among groups of participants may underestimate the effectiveness of treatments for particular individuals. Despite considerable reason to doubt the efficacy of antidepressant drugs, we report these conclusions with a word of caution because it is possible that medication may work for a particular depressed patient and could even be the treatment of choice (Hollon, DeRubeis, Shelton, & Weiss, 2002). While at this stage of our knowledge there is scant support for drugs, it is possible that some drugs have beneficial results for some people. What is abundantly clear is that the small effect sizes found in the treatment studies most certainly do not warrant the aggressive marketing campaigns engineered by the pharmaceutical companies that present antidepressant medications as more effective than the scientific data support. Given the limited effectiveness demonstrated with mild and moderately depressed patients, the common practice of primary care physicians prescribing antidepressant medications to patients who report some depressed symptoms, or who have experienced a negative life event like the loss of a loved one, is highly questionable. As you will see from material presented in later chapters, there is better reason to argue that prescribing psychotherapy, particularly behavioral activation therapy or cognitive-behavioral therapy, should be the first-line treatment, and that primary care physicians should refer to a psychologist, psychiatrist, social worker, or counselor adequately trained in such techniques.

Are Antidepressant Medications Safe?

Since the real story is that the studies of antidepressant medications show only moderate effect sizes compared to the grand statements made in marketing, one wonders whether it is worth taking antidepressants at all. We know that many individuals do report feeling better when they are on medication. As our research review has shown, there is plenty of reason to believe that far fewer patients are responding to the active components of the drug than to the placebo effect of being on a drug. However, if the drugs are safe and non–habit forming, why worry? With this question in mind, we turn to the question of the safety of antidepressant medications.

Side Effects

Although severe side effects were reported by the drug companies as infrequent with the tricyclic antidepressants, in fact they routinely produce side effects that make them difficult for many patients to tolerate. Furthermore, tricyclic antidepressants, and monoamine oxidase inhibitors are potentially lethal if taken in overdose. Antidepressant medications are the most common agent involved in suicide by drug overdose (Kapur, Mieczkowski, & Mann, 1992). The SSRIs may be less likely to be lethal if taken in overdose. However, there is a finding with children and with adults that SSRIs increase suicidal thinking and impulses in some individuals. In his 2000 book, *Prozac Backlash: Overcoming the Dangers of Prozac, Zoloft, Paxil, and Other Antidepressants with Safe, Effective Alternatives*, Dr. Joseph Glenmullen reports many published and anecdotal case studies of SSRIs in which adults had increased agitation, suicidality, or homicidal urges. The possibility of adverse side effects that take many years to develop should be a matter of particular concern when it comes to the use of these drugs by children and adolescents. The drugs they are taking are powerful agents, being taken at a time in their lives when their brains and bodies are still developing. They have many more years of life ahead of them, offering opportunity for the expression of unknown effects that might only show up years later.

The FDA initially reviewed the reports of increased suicidal behavior in adults in 1991 and concluded that there was no basis for the claims that Prozac increased lethality (as reported and critiqued in Glenmullen, 2000). However, in March 2004, the FDA changed its position and requested that a warning for physicians be placed on labels of Prozac (fluoxetine), Zoloft (sertraline), Paxil (paroxetine), Luvox (fluvoxamine), Celexa (citalopram), Lexapro (escitalopram), Wellbutrin (bupropion), Effexor (venlafaxine), Serzone (nefazodone), and Remeron (mirtazapine), urging them to closely observe adult and pediatric patients being treated with these medications for "worsening of depression or the emergence of suicidality" (U.S. Food and Drug Administration, 2004). Given the potential dangers and the questionable efficacy of these drugs, the readiness of primary care physicians to write these prescriptions is ill advised.

A particularly alarming aspect of the problem has to do with the FDA's diminished capacity to monitor the safety of drugs once approved. A 1992 agreement between the FDA and the drug industry provided that the industry would give millions of dollars to the FDA to speed up the approval of new drugs. A feature of the agreement led to severe cuts in the availability of FDA funds to monitor the side effects of drugs that had been approved. As a result, there is now widespread agreement that the FDA's "mechanisms for uncovering the dangers of drugs after they have been approved is woefully inadequate." The FDA "now relies almost entirely on the willingness of the drug makers to report problems that crop up after a drug has been approved" (Harris, 2004a). The pharmaceutical industry has demonstrated dubious interest in voluntarily curtailing its profits by such self-monitoring.

Even though suicidality or homicidal tendencies should not be of grave concern for most people taking antidepressant medications, other side effects are consistently underestimated by the drug companies. The advantage of SSRIs over older antidepressant drugs in lessened production of side effects is marginal. Diarrhea, nausea, insomnia, headaches, and sexual problems are common. On rarer occasions, taking SSRIs has also led to liver damage, seizures, and a condition called akathisia, which is terrible tension that can produce suicidal and homicidal impulses. Numerous lawsuits have been filed against drug companies claiming that taking SSRIs precipitated suicides and murders (Glenmullen, 2000, pp. 161, 173). Breggin and Cohen (2001) compiled a list of 48 reported side effects of Prozac based on the product label. One phenomenon that is not reported on product labels, but is found in most studies comparing medication to therapy, is that more participants in the medication arm of studies tend to drop out than in either the placebo or psychotherapy conditions (Antonuccio, Danton, and DeNelsky, 1995), suggesting that patients taking medication dislike the treatment or neglect to comply with the treatment more than patients who receive psychotherapy. The underestimation by the drug companies of adverse side effects of antidepressant drugs has been substantial. For example, Lilly's literature reports that 2 to 5 percent suffer sexual side effects from Prozac, whereas many studies indicate that 60 percent experience significant sexual side effects (Glenmullen, 2000). Similarly, the literature on Paxil reports adverse side effects in 2 percent of users, when studies suggest the true figure to be anywhere from 20 percent to 60 percent. Unfortunately, the FDA's failure to monitor satisfactorily the side effects of approved drugs has made the full extent of the problems with these antidepressants largely unknown. Because of their concern with adverse side effects, the British regulatory panel that instigated the reevaluation of the use of antidepressants with children because of increased risk of suicidal behavior, has now advised doctors not to prescribe antidepressants "to about 70 percent of the patients who show up complaining of depression," but to try psychotherapy instead or to wait it out (Vedantam, 2004b).

Antonuccio and Naylor (2005) have recently reviewed the literature with regard to the risks associated with taking psychotropic medications. They state that "it is impossible to ignore the fact that antidepressants are not medically benign treatments" (p. 213). Medical risks (including the risk of dying) and side effects of these drugs increase when the use of these drugs is combined with other medications, which is common. And, while the jury is still out and they call for more research, they warn that there is reason to be concerned about a possible association between the SSRIs and breast cancer, self-injurious behavior, manic episodes, and the creation of irreversible biochemical effects that predispose to chronic depression.

Withdrawal

Withdrawal is another issue of concern. Not infrequently, when people attempt to withdraw from antidepressant drugs they experience distressing emotional reactions. And, not infrequently, people misinterpret their distress as a recurrence of their problems caused by going off the medication. This leads them to return to full usage of the drug because they do not recognize their response to be a withdrawal effect. As a result, there is reason to be concerned that many people have become chemically and psychologically dependent on these drugs. And this is not a small matter. Withdrawal effects are so common that the drug companies, because of the negative implications to the term, have invented a euphemism called "discontinuation syndrome" and have urged doctors to use this term rather than "withdrawal" when speaking with patients. A number of journal articles have been published discussing withdrawl problems associated with antidepressants (Coupland, Bell, & Potokar, 1996; Fava, 2002; Rosenbaum, Fava, Hood, Ashcroft, & Krebs, 1998).

Psychological Side Effects

Another kind of side effect should be of concern—a negative psychological side effect. The FDA has warned that some children's suicidal tendencies have been found to be directly attributable to the antidepression medications. Children who experience these reactions do not experience them in a vacuum. Their suicidal behavior occurs as a reaction to intolerable emotional pain and self-hate. Some children on these medications choose death as the solution, and these are the children who are singled out by this warning. Others, however, who choose to live, are not spared. Their emotional development very often is colored by a negative sense of themselves as needing a drug to be like everyone else. Many of these children contend with a self-image of impairment because they have been told and have come to believe that they need a drug to be able to function. This only compounds the difficulties adolescence presents.

Such reactions are commonly seen in adults on medication who come to see themselves as defective because they "need" a drug. It is easy for them to conclude from being diagnosed as having abnormal brain chemistry requiring correction by a medicine that they are different from normal people, who can trust their brains to function properly. Their dependency on the drug often is one of the ingredients undermining their self-worth. For others, reflecting this negative implication, it is not unusual to hear that they wish to get off drugs not only because of the undesirable physical side effects, but because of the psychological side effects that they find abhorrent. In later chapters we discuss effective methods of psychotherapy that spare people from being saddled with such negative baggage and instead offer opportunities for enhanced self-esteem.

Summing Up

In the final analysis, it is the responsibility of every person to question the wisdom of taking an antidepressant or allowing their children to take such medications. Sanguine ideas that one can live a better life through chemistry are not justified given these data. Quite clearly, not everyone will be helped by an antidepressant, and those reporting feeling better only feel better while they remain on the drug. Research suggests that reports of feeling better most likely are attributable to a placebo effect. There may or may not be noxious side effects, but there is always the ominous possibility that some side effects will show up much later and could be serious (there are historical examples with previously prescribed drugs of negative effects that were irreversible). Such factors as the therapeutic relationship have a significant impact on the effectiveness of all treatments for depression, including medication (Krupnick, Sotsky, Elkin, Watkins, & Pilkonis, 1996). Therefore, it is even less likely that getting refills for medication over the phone from a primary care doctor will help without the ongoing relationship with a psychologist, psychiatrist, psychiatric nurse practitioner, counselor, or social worker. Even such simple things as exercise have been shown to either be as effective as both medication or psychotherapy, or to improve the efficacy of these treatments (Norden, 1995), suggesting that it is never a good idea to simply accept depression as an illness that one needs to passively take a pill to cure. Since there are also no happy pills for children, parents will continue to struggle with moody or irritable children without a surefire panacea.

While medications may produce effects that are comparable to psychotherapy, studies suggest that psychotherapy has more enduring effects. We have much more to say about this in Chapter 6. Interpersonal therapy produces greater improvement in overall quality of life, and cognitive-behavior therapy does better in prevention of relapse (Hollon, DeRubeis, Shelton, & Weiss, 2002). When it comes to the treatment of depression, Joseph Glenmullen (2000) has expressed caution well: "The term 'antidepressant' is misleading because it implies a definitive treatment for a definitive condition, neither of which is the case" (p. 215). It is important to know that the data suggest a variety of alternatives in treatment. Equally important is knowing that psychiatric diagnoses for such disorders as depression and anxiety are not perfect when conducted by the most skilled therapists. The diagnosis is even less likely to be adequate when made by a primary care physician who is a generalist with very little training in psychiatry or psychology.

CHAPTER 3

THE CONTEXT OF
DEPRESSION AND ANXIETY

Biological Explanations

Biological explanations of the cause of psychological problems are insufficient at best. Like any theory that looks at only one factor, the biological theory overlooks too many other factors. Far too little is accounted for. If depression is caused by a "chemical imbalance" in the brain, what causes the chemical imbalance? Diagnoses of depression have tripled since World War II. Millions of prescriptions are written for antidepressant medications each year. Such an increase would suggest that there is a nationwide epidemic of depression. How could this be explained? Has there been a genetic mutation that has occurred in the twentieth century that has spurred a rash of chemical imbalances?

Such reasoning points out several problems with the current state of the mental health field. First, a simple notion about chemical imbalances clearly does not explain what causes or maintains depression. Second, many of the millions of prescriptions written every year are written for people who may be distressed but who don't meet diagnostic criteria for clinical depression. Third, as discussed in Chapter 1, the diagnostic system that is used is vague, filled with overlapping descriptions, and lacks reliability. In short, there is more to the explanation of depression that is accounted for by other theories than a simple medical model.

It's Not Your Brain, It's Your Life

A comprehensive understanding of depression or any other emotional problem is accounted for in the biopsychosocial model. This model considers biological, psychological, and sociological factors that contribute to human emotions. Although implied by the word, biology does not come first, however. In fact, a contextual model states that all emotion and behavior must be considered in a given context. Some people who are depressed report that they feel blue "all of the time." This is a common perception among people who feel predominantly depressed. However, when most people evaluate their lives in more detail, they find that there are some times when they feel better than other times. Let's take an example, grief after the loss of a loved one. One can observe the behavior of a grief-stricken family attending a wake and funeral services. If you observe any person at the service and throughout the course of the day there will be moments when they are tearful and solemn. At other moments they may be pensively engaged in conversation with others attending the services as they talk about the loss of quality of life in the final months of the life of their loved one. There may be times when they smile or laugh when someone reminisces about happy times or a humorous event in the life of the deceased. Although, on the whole, the person is still suffering with grief, he or she is not experiencing the same manifestation of it at all times throughout the day. Moods shift, sometimes ever so slightly and at other times dramatically, as the context shifts.

By context we mean the situation in which a behavior occurs (the who, when, what, and where), the biological state of the person, his or her private thoughts and feelings that develop over the course of life, and the consequences that occur when the person acts one way or another, which determine what is learned from experience. Let's take an example from current events. The world was recently shocked to learn that Iraqi prisoners of war were being abused by U.S. guards in the Abu Ghraib prison, allegedly acting deviantly beyond their orders. Whether or not they were following orders, many Americans ask, "How could this happen?" Reductionistic views would relate the reason to a chemical imbalance in the brains of the guards, or to "learned violent personalities," or to some other simplistic explanation. However, none of these explanations tells the whole story.

We know from studies in the 1960s and 1970s (Milgram, 1963; and for a recent accounting of earlier experiments, Zimbardo, 2004) that average college students with no prior history of mental illness or violent behavior will follow orders to administer what they believed to be painful shocks to other participants (as in the Milgram study) or turn into violent and abusive prison guards in a prison simulation (Zimbardo). Many variables in the shifting context account for the behavior of the guards in Iraq, whether they were deviating from their orders or not. After all, even if they were following orders, they were engaged in behaviors that most would regard as reprehensible. Simple explanations for peoples' behavior, even when they sound "scientific" and seemingly grounded in an appeal to biological and neurological processes, are inadequate.

Learning Takes Place in a Context

Conditioning studies that are described in the next chapter provide an important part of the explanation. Considering conditioning alone, however, would also be reductionistic. The process of conditioning accounts for why certain behavior patterns are continued in similar circumstances (because they are reinforced) or conversely why certain behaviors are discontinued (because they go without reinforcement or are punished). Yet understanding behavioral conditioning does not account for changes beneath the skin that occur as a result of shifting context. There is abundant evidence that behavioral processes are affected by biological processes and that biological processes are affected by behavioral processes. For example, in the early 1970s, a study revealed that women living together as college students in a dormitory became synchronized in their menstrual cycles. The study also revealed that the length of their periods was directly related to the amount of time they interacted with men. Social factors mediated biology by means of the mechanism of the scent of underarm perspiration (McClintock, 1971; McClintock & Stern, 1998).

While much has been made of how behavior (depression, for example) is determined by neurotransmitters, there is as much reason to believe that neurotransmitters like serotonin and norepinephrine are affected by behavioral acts. Whenever you think about a past event, or when you move your legs to walk, something changes in your brain. When a danger is present, the brain reacts by sending messages to the nerves throughout the body to protect you, a signal rushes blood to the extremities, and the muscles become tense. Learning takes place in response to those signals and in response to the salient environmental cues. We have some reason to believe that levels of neurotransmitters are associated with shifting moods. However, as noted in Chapter 2, there are no clear data to indicate that increases or decreases in neurotransmitter levels cause depression, result from it, or reflect some other process basic to both.

Avoidance

At this point in our understanding of depression, the most powerful explanation we have comes from behavioral research, which has led to the concept of avoidance behavior. Central to both depression and anxiety is a process referred to as avoidance, which has a specific technical description in behavioral psychology. Unlike the serotonin theory, this theory has solid backing in research, which is outlined in some detail in Chapter 4. When psychologists speak of avoidance, we are not just describing a conscious act, such as swerving out of the way of an oncoming vehicle to avoid a collision. Avoidance is defined as a behavior that is maintained by the consequences of its occurrence. Take a simple example of a person who dislikes a colleague. When he overhears others talking positively about this colleague he finds himself stirred up. By walking away he feels better, less upset. His increased blood pressure, feelings of anger, hurt, and anxiety-laden impulses to criticize his colleague all are reduced by walking away. This is an example of avoidance behavior; by leaving the situation that was giving rise to his distress, he felt better. Simple behaviors of this sort to reduce negative emotions can have significant consequences, as is outlined in Chapter 5. There are times when avoidance behavior is functional, and there are times when it is dysfunctional—leading to conditions that are diagnosed as mental disorder. Avoidance behavior is readily learned, quite common, and a powerful feature that accounts for a great deal of dysfunctional human behavior. It develops and recurs in a biopsychosocial context.

Avoidance behavior has been studied extensively for many years. Its central role in accounting for anxiety disorders is now very well established. What has been slower to be understood is the relevance of this research to depression. Chapter 4 gives the science behind this conceptualization, and Chapter 5 provides illustrations of how a behavior therapist uses this concept in treatment.

How Life Stressors, Even from Early Childhood, Can Lead to Patterns of Avoidance

Avoidance learning is a subtle process with varied manifestations that begins early in life. Adverse life conditions, particularly in childhood when personal resources are more limited and dependency is a reality, are more likely to lead to learning avoidance behavior. Imagine a child who comes from the kind of home where the parents fight frequently and violently. The child may complain of being frightened, but this does not stop the fighting. Under such circumstances, the child may learn to comfort herself by retreating to her room and by telling a doll "I'm scared" as a way of comforting herself. If this becomes an established pattern in conflict situations, then the child will go into isolation to comfort herself instead of engaging with the environment, and an avoidance pattern will have been learned that inhibits problem-solving. Children with this kind of history come to respond to their own sense of deprivation or fear by not readily engaging with their environment for solutions. This is particularly the case when parents fail to recognize a child is in distress or fail to teach the child problem-solving behaviors when distressed. Behavioral psychologists (Ferster, 1973) have described this type of pattern as a possible pathway to developing depressed behaviors later in life.

Avoidance learning is promoted in other ways. When a situation calls for a high amount of activity for a low level of reward, continuing to make the effort is discouraged. A person may develop a pattern of behaving in ways that reduce discomfort rather than in ways that engage with the environment to attain a desired goal. In adults we can see this type of pattern, for example, when a lonely man who feels sad because he does not have companionship tries to date, but he never meets anyone appropriate or he lacks the social skills to make a good connection. After a while he stops his pursuit to find a partner, instead taking to his bed for many hours a day or drinking alcohol alone in his house. Sleeping and drinking provide temporary relief from his distress. These two behaviors are being maintained by avoidance. In other words, the more sleeping or drinking removes a negative experience, in this case his sadness and loneliness and fear of failure, the more likely he is to be avoidant. As a result, his aloneness increases, and the negative emotions increase. If, in his attempts to date, he had met someone who became either a romantic partner or a good friend, his social behavior would have been positively reinforced and he would be more likely to continue engaging in social activities.

Behaviors such as sleeping excessively, drinking alcohol or taking drugs, overeating, or even complaining to friends frequently are escape or avoidance behaviors. They allow one to either escape from negative feelings and activities or avoid having to engage in something that is distressing. These are not the behaviors of deviant people who are different from the rest of humankind. Everyone engages in escape or avoidance behavior. Avoidance is a mechanism that is natural, ubiquitous, and has profound implications in shaping human behavior.

Avoidance Can Be Adaptive

People avoid accidents all of the time by stopping at posted stop signs or traffic signals. Except in driver's training, when the instructor may say "good job" and thereby positively reinforce stopping at red lights or "No, watch out!" as a punishing exclamation, the behavior of stopping at traffic signals is maintained by avoidance. If you stop, you don't get into an accident or get a ticket; hence, the problem is avoided.

Avoidance behaviors have functional value when the behavior being avoided is truly dangerous. Stopping at a stop sign is avoidance behavior that is likely to prevent a negative consequence. Such avoidance has adaptive value, probably accounting for the existence of the physiological system. However, many avoidance behaviors in everyday life block the learning of functional behavior. Sometimes, as in responding to a stop sign, avoidance is valuable, but at other times the avoidance interferes with one's life. A clear-cut illustration of this is found in phobias, where for example, avoidance of flying prevents a person from unlearning the fear and being able to travel.

Avoidance and Anxiety

Survival is guaranteed by being able to outfight, outrun, or outsmart one's predators and opponents. All mammals experience something akin to fear. Watch any nature channel on television and you are likely to see "panicked" herds of antelope running from lions or "fearful" monkeys looking this way and that for a snake in a tree. Fear causes mammals to do one of three things: fight, flee, or freeze.

The automatic response, often referred to as the fight or flight response, is absolutely necessary when a species is being pursued by other species that have stronger muscles, bigger teeth, and view them as a tasty dinner. In the type of environment in which the human species evolved, such responses were essential for survival. If people needed to stop and think about a game plan before making a decision to get out of the way of a charging lion, there would most likely not be any people left to populate the planet. Instead, instantaneous responses evolved to escape from danger or avoid it altogether. When there is potentially a tiger in the brush, hearing a twig break, looking closely and nervously into the darkness ahead, and deciding to walk quickly in the other direction could help avoid being eaten. Humans, however, because we have developed societies far more advanced than our evolutionary history has allowed adaptation for, now experience problems traceable to the triggering of these fight, flight, or freeze responses that are no longer suited to our daily lives, with the possible exception of small tribal groups such as the Masai in Eastern Africa.

The emotional experience that accompanies detection of danger is called fear or anxiety. It doesn't matter whether the danger is objectively real or not. What matters is our interpretation. The sound of a twig snapping under the weight of a pig if interpreted as caused by a tiger leads to fear and flight. Similarly, for humans, if a grasshopper is interpreted as dangerous, anxiety and flight occurs regardless of the objective nature of the situation. There is a spiraling effect to anxiety that contributes to its power in promoting action. Experts in anxiety have described how problems are worsened by the spiraling effect of the combination of life events, internal experience, our interpretations of events, and learned avoidant behaviors. If an individual experiences anxiety or uncomfortable bodily symptoms in one situation (such as heart palpitations when driving over a bridge), he or she may then begin to dread a recurrence of these feelings and to avoid not only bridges but other situations that elicit similar negative emotions. The avoidance of such situations increases the dread, which leads to more avoidance (Craske & Barlow, 2000). This process is the hallmark of phobic disorders, and when the dread is attached to the anxiety response, panic disorders occur. Generalized anxiety also works in this fashion, although much of the avoidance behavior is manifest in the form of worries.

Worries can serve as avoidance because they bring no solution to a problem. Worrying can be seen as problem-solving gone awry (Norman Cotterell, personal communication, 1999). Rather than coming to an appropriate solution and then carrying out the steps, people with generalized anxiety disorder—colloquially characterized as "worriers"—work the problem over and over in their mind, imagining catastrophic outcomes. The fear paralyzes them from taking steps toward solutions. The worrying substitutes for taking action by thinking about the problem but not doing anything about it. Consequently, worrying is avoidance behavior.

Avoidance is most obvious in phobias. A young man who is afraid of heights will go out of his way to avoid crossing a bridge, walking up a ladder, or looking over the edge of a skyscraper deck. People with phobic fear of dogs cross to the other side of the street when they approach someone walking a large pet; people with snake phobias refuse to go through tall grass; claustrophobic people will not meet someone in an office that has no window; those afraid of elevators take stairs; and the list goes on.

The important point is that avoidance behavior is rooted in the immediate consequences of its occurrence, which had value for primitive man, but in modern-day life, immediate relief often yields a dysfunctional solution because the long-term consequences are negative. Fear of flying may be solved by deciding not to fly, but because there often are worthwhile reasons to travel by air, the long-term consequences are unfortunate. Research, and in many ways common sense, tells us that the best way to conquer a fear is to face it, and an abundant literature in psychology describes how fears can be conquered by exposure rather than avoidance (Foa & Kozak, 1986). The mechanism governing avoidance behavior is called negative reinforcement, which is discussed in the next chapter.

Extinction

What happens in all of the anxiety disorders is this: Upon encountering the feared situation, anxiety begins to rise. Studies have shown that if the individual were to stay in contact with the feared stimulus, the anxiety would reach a peak and then begin to abate in a process called habituation. Extinction (which also is discussed in more detail in the next chapter) and habituation are related. Habituation and extinction describe how a response diminishes with repeated exposures to a stimulus without reinforcement. The point is, if a person can be enabled to stay in a feared situation long enough, his or her fears will diminish.

The problem is that it is very difficult to stay with something one fears. It doesn't matter much that other people deal with such situations without difficulty. Most people with anxiety disorders leave the situation in one way or another at a point during which their fear is rising. Thus, the escape response (avoidance) is reinforced by the reduction in the painful experience of fear. In fact, the learned fear may even have increased because the individual has had another exposure to fear but has not remained in contact long enough with the feared stimulus to experience reduced anxiety because of habituation.

The behavioral therapies described in Chapter 6 are strategies for helping people deal more effectively with this problem.

The Compelling Nature of Fear

What makes it so hard to stay in a situation in which one is afraid? When it comes to avoidance behaviors that are regarded as disorders, one can offer the psychological or cognitive explanation that a person is anticipating greater danger than is truly present. Regardless of how one accounts for the negative emotional state, perhaps surprisingly, the truest answer is that the person is afraid because of avoidance. Consider what is taking place for such a person: Once avoidance learning takes place, the individual—in that context, with those internal stimuli—is now reacting very importantly to him- or herself in that situation. It is ironic that the avoidance behavior is maintaining the problem rather than relieving it. Successful therapy depends on finding means to enable continued contact with the feared stimulus rather than avoidance in order for the avoidance behavior to be unlearned and more functional behavior learned in its place. Learning how to respond successfully requires staying in the situation. Often it is the case that recognizing that one already knows how to respond successfully also requires staying in the situation. The good news is that there is an emotional payoff for finding the courage to do this. Overcoming the fear increases self-confidence. A person with a fear of heights, who through a series of therapeutic efforts overcomes that fear, often experiences a giddy sense of increased self-regard.

Getting over the Hump

In everyday life, when a person tries to stay in a feared situation without getting the reinforcement provided by escape, the fear will at first increase. It is natural, therefore, to want to escape and the pressure to escape will increase before extinction occurs. This is why people who are afraid to speak in public may back out of a commitment the night before a talk, someone who is shy and socially withdrawn will sit alone in a corner at a party or avoid the party altogether, and so on. The increase in fear as the individual approaches the situation increases the desire to get out of the situation.

Unfortunately, in our "brave new world," physicians often prescribe anti-anxiety agents or antidepressants to alleviate the feelings of anxiety. When a socially phobic person takes Paxil and attends a party because he or she feels less anxious, there is temporary success, but extinction of the fear is not occurring. The individual learns to rely on the medication as a crutch. A crutch for a broken leg is well understood to be wise only as a temporary measure. Unlike crutches that are readily discarded when no longer necessary, medication crutches often are prescribed as the cure. Even when they are suggested as a means toward behavioral change, there is reason to be concerned about the effectiveness of this strategy. The prescription is couched in terms of having an illness that requires medical treatment. Unfortunately, what is really happening is that the medication blocks the curative process. While the medication-induced reduction in anxiety may increase the likelihood of engaging in a feared activity, it is not curative if one is looking for stable, long-term change. If the same person learns methods to get through the extinction curve, letting the anxiety rise until it ultimately is extinguished, there is the likelihood of lasting change coming about as a result of the person's own efforts—a change that is likely to generalize to other anxiety-provoking situations.

People who can face a fear because their anxiety has been medicated away come to see themselves as having an illness that is treated with medication. The same can be said for people who face a fear because they are holding a magical charm, are accompanied by a "therapy dog," or approach the situation only in the company of a close friend. All of these are considered safety behaviors that therapists working with anxious people help their clients to discontinue. Although a person may first face the feared situation with a friend, a therapist, or under the treatment of a medication, all of those safety factors need to be faded out in order for the person to make lasting change in reducing his or her avoidance behavior and dependency on others or some agent. Those people who learn methods of facing a fear and experience the fear diminishing by dint of their efforts alone will be more likely to celebrate their strengths and to no longer see themselves as ill. They are able to say, "I have this or that anxiety, now I know successful ways of engaging in the activity anyway, and as a result I feel better about myself." Skilled therapists help their clients work up to the ultimate experience of facing the fear. We are not suggesting that people need to "just do it" and jump into anxiety-producing situations by gritting their teeth and enduring unimaginable fear. Rather, there are methods for learning to approach fear that make use of relaxation procedures, evaluating beliefs about the feared object, and systematically working through increasingly difficult situations that have helped many people to permanently overcome fear and avoidance.

The Concept of Depression

It should be clear now how anxiety and fear have an evolutionary basis that is not always functional for us in the modern world. It is less understandable how depression could ever be adaptive. There are no satisfactory theories of the evolutionary basis for depression, although some have been proposed. It seems more likely that for the great bulk of people who experience mild or moderate depression, their depression is not a basic mechanism, as is the case with fear and anxiety. Rather, the enormous increase in the diagnosis of depression is the result of the current extraordinary marketing and prescribing of drugs. Our pill-crazy culture that seeks happiness in prescription bottles has provided a ready audience.

Sadness and disappointment are normal reactions in life that ordinarily are temporary. Depression occurs when these states become long-term. Depression is better conceptualized as a mood state that can be induced by anxiety-driven responses, particularly avoidance responses. Two ingredients are common in this process: (1) self-negation and (2) avoidance of engaging in those behaviors that are necessary to overcome elements that are at the heart of the sadness. Of these two factors, avoidance of the behaviors is by far more important to the continuation of depression. Medication is directed at changing self-negation—that is, essentially the mood-state per se. Even in those instances when avoidance is prevented by taking medication, the effects are state-dependent. Corrective action is contingent upon the induction of an artificial state; the person is "hooked." Thus, whatever positive effects accrue to taking drugs disappear when the drugs are discontinued. Similarly, psychotherapies that are directed simply at self-negation—that is, toward enabling the person to feel better about him- or herself—are equally ineffective because the results also will be temporary. The curative psychotherapies are those that are directed primarily or even sometimes exclusively at avoidance because the result of the self-generation of corrective actions often leads to self-negation taking care of itself.

Grief

Depression often resembles grief, which probably is more basic since it is relatively easy to make a case for its value in life. When a person one loves is injured, departs, or dies, one grieves. Grief includes feeling sad, crying, perhaps being short-tempered and irritable, longing for the person for whom one grieves, and so on. Intense grief reactions are characterized by terribly painful waves of emotion. When one cares deeply for someone, one grieves deeply. If we did not feel grief over loss, it would be quite easy to become expendable to one another. Mothers could toss their babies away with no shame or sadness. If we wanted an annoying spouse out of the way, we could just kill him or her. In other words, we would be a society full of sociopaths who do not experience what we colloquially refer to as "pangs of conscience." This would, indeed, be maladaptive. Grief has survival value. It is our emotional reaction to loss, rooted in love and attachment. The death of a loved one naturally causes grief over the loss of the presence of that person and all the behaviors connected to that person. The grief response can be more complicated when there has been important dependency on a loved one who has died. Depression may result if that loss triggers feelings of helplessness and avoidance of learning independence. Similarly, break-ups of relationships may trigger simply grief or they may trigger other emotions and responses that are inducers of depression. If the sense of loss is accompanied by self-depreciation or fear of new relationships, avoidance and depression are more likely.

Shame

It is not unusual for depression to develop when there has been loss together with a negative self-attribution that fuels avoidance. It is the avoidance in this context that compounds the problem of loss and leads to depression. If one loses a job, a relationship, or a goal and blames oneself for what has occurred in a way that interferes with good, functional activity to recover from the loss, depression often results. The avoidance behaviors can be fueled by a sense of shame or failure that interfere with behaviors that would provide access to some desirable replacement for the loss. The fact that others may place no blame on the person for the setbacks often makes no impact. Each of us responds to our own context, not someone else's.

Our society is very competitive, with great emphasis placed on material and social success. Rags to riches and lifting oneself by one's bootstraps reflect the American Dream. Our mass media give vivid exposure to models of great success. Is it any wonder that those who fall short of their dreams would experience feelings of depression, particularly when there is awareness of avoidance behavior as having limited their success relative to others with whom they compare themselves? Are people who have interpreted their lives in this way supposed to feel good about themselves?

The process, however, is not a simple one. Many variables come into play, including the age of onset when one first experiences feelings of depression. It may be that early loss, before a child has developed good coping behaviors, sets the stage for the later dysfunctional response. Early loss of a parent for women and early childhood health problems for men have been shown to predict later depression (Reinherz et al., 1999). Recent romantic break-ups are associated with the onset of first episodes of depression in adolescents (Monroe, Rohde, Seeley, & Lewinsohn, 1999). This may well be the result of more fragile egos at this time in life that make negative self-attributions more common. It is interesting that children of parents who are divorcing, which is perceived by many as a time of loss, differentially react to the divorce. In other words, the divorce of parents per se is not correlated with the onset of depression in children, but factors such as mother's income, education, ethnicity, depressive symptoms, and behavior were associated with depression in the children (Clarke-Stewart, Vandell, McCartney, Owen, & Booth, 2000). The effects of the mother's behavior probably is due to the fact that children most often are placed with their mothers following the separation or divorce of parents. So, although there are not direct connections between any particular life experiences and depression, data have consistently shown that people who experience negative life events, what some have referred to as "fateful loss events" (Shrout et al., 1989), are more likely to suffer from depression.

Co-morbidity

Following the paradigm of anxiety, it is not the reaction to negative life events in itself that is usually a problem, but rather the reaction to the reaction. In fact, the medical literature has cited a connection between depression and anxiety. In this literature, the term "co-morbidity" is used when a patient has two or more medical disorders at the same time. Without reiterating our displeasure with the medical model, the psychiatric and psychological literature suggests that there may be as high as 55 percent co-occurrence of one or more anxiety disorders or of anxiety and depression (Barlow, Allen, & Choate, 2004). In other words, over half of people who are suffering from depression are also diagnosed as suffering from some type of anxiety disorder. With such high co-occurrence rates, it becomes increasingly difficult to make definitive statements about two distinct "disorders." Furthermore, evidence suggests that a general emotional factor characterized by anxious apprehension, narrowed attention, and reduced autonomic reactivity characterizes people diagnosed with both depressive and anxiety disorders (Chorpita & Barlow, 1998). Escape and avoidance behavior appears to be as much a part of the onset of depression as it is in the anxiety disorders.

Several investigators have pointed to avoidance behaviors as relevant to depression. More than 30 years ago, Ferster pointed out that the type of inertia seen in depression may itself, in fact, be avoidance behavior (Ferster, 1973). We have also discussed how worry is often avoidance; that is, it is problem-solving gone awry. Such thinking is often characteristic of depression. People with passive, repetitive thinking styles tend to be more depressed and to stay depressed longer than those who use active coping (Nolen-Hoeksema, Morrow, & Frederickson, 1993). Ruminative thinking about one's problems—such as worrying—may serve as escape and avoidance behavior. One may ask, "How is that avoiding, since it feels terrible to dwell on one's problems?" We would point to the function that the behavior serves rather than whether it is pleasant or unpleasant. Thinking about one's problems may serve to reduce some of the distress of those problems. Certainly, "shutting down" by staying in bed for long periods of time, disengaging from activities that once provided pleasure, and withdrawing socially all can serve as a form of numbing oneself from the distress one feels.

Take job loss as an example, and it is a good example because it is often a precursor to depression in adults. During a time of an economic downswing when jobs are hard to find, it takes a great deal of effort to look for employment. One may need to complete multiple applications prior to getting even one interview. Even then, the interview process, which is stressful, may not yield a job. Over time, it is understandable how a person would begin to doubt the utility of his or her efforts, come to experience self-doubt, and decrease the job search. Decreased effort inevitably leads to continued joblessness, validating self-deprecatory views and further inhibiting job-seeking efforts. At the same time, it would also be understandable that one would continue to worry about not having a job and depleting one's savings. Demoralized by the loss of social status, worried about finances, any number of escape and avoidance behaviors such as sleep, alcohol or drug use, or watching television easily can come to outnumber active job searching. The person will find him- or herself in the downward spiral of depression.

Negative Belief Systems in Depression

Depression is often characterized by negative thinking and devaluation of oneself. As in anxiety, there may be an overestimation of potential harm that causes one to be wary and apprehensive. In depression, one may have a tendency to attribute problems to failures in the self that are fixed and stable. In other words, one may begin to see oneself as a "failure" or a "loser." This type of thinking can, in turn, lead to decreases in coping behavior. Again, this is the crucial factor: avoidance of engaging in the behaviors that are called for as a consequence of negative feelings about self. When thinking about going for a job interview leads to anxiety over anticipated failure and causes the person to avoid the interview, the seeds are present for depression to develop. As the negative valuation of the self continues, hopelessness ensues. Hopelessness has been correlated with greater intensity of depression and with suicidal behaviors (Beck, Resnick, & Lettieri, 1986). Thus, the hopelessness, lethargy, ruminative thinking, and general inertia continue to keep a person locked in a continuing spiral into depression that feels more and more "physical" to him or her. It may be that significant life events and this downward spiral also have an impact on the levels of neurotransmitters in the brain, but there is no good reason to believe that the problem started there.

Putting on a Happy Face

Several investigators have discussed the problem with something that has been referred to as experiential avoidance (Hayes, Strosahl, & Wilson, 1999; Kohlenberg & Tsai, 1991). This is the process of blunting, ignoring, distracting from, medicating, or otherwise trying to escape from negative feelings and/or the negative consequences of our behavior. Instead of accepting our emotions as a part of our lives and learning to act constructively with them, we have a tendency to try to make ourselves feel better at any cost. Once again, marketing has had a great impact on this. There was once a time when suffering was thought to be a part of life. People did not expect to feel happiness and joy on a continual basis. With the advent of the twentieth century, however, we have been told that we should get ecstatic about cereal ("cuckoo for Cocoa Puffs"), that every night is a "Michelob night" (that is, a good time to numb ourselves with alcohol), or any number of images of happy groups of people wearing new clothes or having wonderful times on vacations to exotic places. Not that being dour and melancholy is a better alternative, but accepting that life comes with ups and downs is important. One book on depression and anxiety asks in its title "You mean I don't have to feel this way?" (Dowling, 1993) and accuses nonmedical mental health professionals of obstructing treatment by not properly pointing their clients toward medication treatments. The understandable desperation one can feel when life is overwhelming can make many people wish to find a magic bullet cure. If only the antidepressants, mood stabilizers, and anti-anxiety agents were indeed magic, there might be justification for all the hype, but, as we have reviewed, the literature on efficacy does not bear that out.

Wanting to escape from negative experiences can lead to many problems. Psychoanalysts for years talked about repression and considered it highly problematic and as leading to multiple symptoms. Although behaviorists do not speak in those terms because such abstract phenomena are not easily verified empirically, it is still clear that one may replace adaptive with maladaptive behaviors in order to avoid the negative experiences of life. In order not to feel scared, one often has to restrict one's movements; not to feel hurt, one may choose to avoid getting involved in close relationships; to avoid feeling rejected, one may not pursue goals. Keeping oneself in safe situations, socially isolated or underemployed, may allow one to avoid feeling fearful or overwhelmed, but it can also lead to feeling depressed when life does not work out as one would hope.

There is empirical evidence that emotional avoidance is problematic. Many emotional disorders are the result of attempts to avoid excessive and unexpected emotional experiences (Barlow, Allen, & Choate, 2004). Some examples noted by Barlow and his colleagues are studies of veterans with post-traumatic stress disorder (PTSD) conducted by Roemer, Litz, Orsillo, and Wagner in 2001 (as cited in Barlow, Allen, & Choate, 2004), where veterans with PTSD were more likely to report withholding their emotions than veterans who did not meet criteria for PTSD. Furthermore, Barlow and colleagues refer to the literature on teaching such clients to use calming procedures such as relaxation to cope with panic, a procedure that is now known to be counterproductive in many cases, actually increasing panic. These and many other examples demonstrate that trying to avoid emotional experience causes rather than cures problems.

CHAPTER 4

Psychology as a Science

Scientific Observation

Psychology is a branch of natural science that is defined in terms of its subject matter. The subject matter of psychology is the behavior of organisms. All of the sciences begin with observation, but because scientists cannot observe everything, regardless of the branch of science much depends on what scientists think is important. Simply observing, however, does not guarantee that objectivity will follow, as the following instances of observer bias illustrate:

> Aristotle held that the vital principle of the embryo comes from the father alone; the role of the mother is confined to supplying the raw materials and nourishing the embryo. This doctrine was held in medieval Europe by Albertus Magnus in the 13th C and with modifications by William Harvey (1651). Some of the microscopists at the beginning of the 18th C convinced themselves that human spermatozoa contain miniature human figures complete with arms, legs, and a head, and they carefully illustrated these so-called homunculi. One of the early microscopists found a microscopic horse in the semen of a horse and a minute fowl in the semen of a cock. (Grant, 1956)
>
> The formulations of Galen were so completely accepted in the Middle Ages that early anatomists, viewing internal organs either through accidents of war or under dissection, simply did not observe or reproduce what contemporary physiologists think they "should" have seen. That is, physiological anomalies consistent with Galenic dicta were observed,

but observations contrary to Galen's doctrines were rationalized as coming from "defective corpses." (Ullman & Krasner, 1969)

Scientific statements are testable. Any science is a set of statements that describe the relationship to one another of the observations of interest to that field. For the psychologist, the task is to devise a scientific account of the behavior of organisms. In studying behavior, psychology seeks to understand the relationships of behavioral variables to the conditions that control them. The measure of a science is the extent to which the statements of that science meet particular criteria. Most important among these criteria is that the statements be objectively testable. It is in this regard that psychoanalysis failed to qualify as a scientific procedure. Its concepts were based on case reports, not controlled experiments. When case reports were published with results that were contradictory to the theory, other publications would follow pointing out how the outcome was predictable from some other facet of the theory. Psychoanalytic theory was so complex and internally inconsistent that no test was possible to verify its principles.

Science is empirical. Statements about what is observed must be made in a form that permits a determination of whether they are true or false. Observations may be made in various ways—for example, reading a dial, noting the positions of the planets in space, reporting changes in color in a test tube, or timing the speed of a rat as it runs through a maze. When such observations are recorded, they become the raw data of science.

The data of science must be communicable. The language of science is very important in that it must be precise enough for observations to be communicated without distortion. This is the primary reason why scientists prefer data that are numerical. Once data are recorded, interpretation is important because science is interested in arriving at an organized, systematic understanding of how observations relate to one another. Hence, a seed catalogue, while filled with explicit data, does not qualify as science.

Laws in Psychology

As outlined in Chapter 1, there is a long history of attempts to comprehend human behavior as it is expressed in various life situations. For psychology, this understanding requires the discovery of the events from which behavior can be predicted, including statements of how behavior depends upon these events. Take for example such sayings

from folklore as "practice makes perfect" or " If at first you don't succeed, try, try again" or the carpenter's rule: "Measure twice, cut once."
These are commonly accepted bits of wisdom about behaviors and outcomes. They arose out of a coalescence of informal, casual observation
and describe cause and effect relationships. They are quite imprecise,
but they are the sort of statements that interests psychologists.

As a science, psychology insists on systematic collection of data
within defined parameters before pronouncements are made about the
relationship of behavior to outcome. Folklore statements are incom-
plete; they lack the precision demanded of a scientific statement. For
example, with regard to "If at first you don't succeed, try, try again,"
there is the implication that continued effort will lead to success, but
there is no specification as to whether effort is a simply necessary or
sufficient condition, there is no identification of what is meant by effort,
what aims may or may not be covered, etc. However, it is a crude example of an attempt to specify a cause and effect relationship. Psychologists seek to make statements with greater rigor (Kimble, 1956).

Statements such as the ones we have been discussing are examples
of stimulus-response (S-R) laws. These are laws that have to do with
responses that are related to some event that precedes the behavior (an
antecedent event). Other statements made by psychologists that relate
behavior in one situation to behavior in another are referred to as
response-response (R-R) laws. When a psychologist administers a test
and uses the test results to predict performance in school, she is demonstrating an R-R relationship. Whether the prediction is in the form
of an S-R statement or an R-R statement, the prediction always has to
do with behavior. There is an important difference in the utility of S-R
and R-R statements to psychologists: while each of them allows for
prediction, S-R statements are more pragmatic because they offer the
possibility of influencing behavior, whereas R-R laws only allow determination of whether behaviors are or are not related. When S-R laws
are known, they have been derived from experimentation.

Experiments and Models

In the design of experiments, two kinds of variables are identified.
The phenomena studied by a given science are called the dependent
variables. For psychology, the behaviors to be predicted or controlled
constitute the dependent variables—that is, the response in the S-R
laws. Behaviors that are diagnosed as mental disorders are dependent

variables. The event or antecedent condition from which the prediction is made is called the independent variable. After the empirical relationships are established, the scientist provides a systematic interpretation to put these observations into a coherent context. Psychologists do this by postulating an intervening variable (a "hypothetical construct"), such as memory or hunger. Because intervening variables are unobservable they must be related to the antecedent events and behavioral events to which they refer. We state that an animal is hungry because we observe that it eats. To be scientific, we should state that an animal is hungry as a result of food deprivation, which is demonstrated by eating behavior. Unless intervening variables can be tied down in this way, subject to testing, they fail to meet the criteria for science. To say that an animal is hungry because it eats and that it eats because it is hungry is circular, because eating and the explanation for it (hunger) are derived from a single set of facts. Similarly, to state that a woman fails to assert herself because she has low self-esteem is not a satisfactory scientific explanation. Psychoanalytic theory is replete with "explanatory" statements of this kind. Absent objectively specifying the antecedent conditions, the statement of the intervening variable does not qualify as acceptable to science.

The basic process of explanation in science is deduction. A phenomenon has been explained if it can be shown to follow from a general principle. The principle of gravity explains the orbits of the planets. When a set of principles is established, a theory is developed to describe the empirical events in that field. This theoretical structure is called a model. Hence, the medical model was derived from application of the scientific method that yielded an understanding of how to control disease. Psychologists are working toward development of a model for understanding and controlling behavior, including the behaviors defined as mental disorders.

Principles of Learning

We know that human behavior is profoundly influenced by learning. In seeking to predict and control behavior, psychologists seek to understand how learning takes place. Learning occurs in an individual when a functional connection is established between a stimulus and the individual's response. A basic premise in psychology is that the behaviors that characterize mental disorder develop in the same way and are maintained in the same way as other learned behaviors.

Dollard and Miller (1950) stated:

Human behavior is learned; precisely that behavior which is widely felt
to characterize man as a rational being, or as a member of a particular
nation or social class, is learned rather than innate. We also learn fears,
guilt, and other socially acquired motivations and symptoms—factors
which are characteristic of normal personality but show up more clearly
in extreme form as mental disorder.

Classical or Respondent Conditioning

Two models of learning have been identified: classical conditioning
(also called respondent or Pavlovian conditioning) and instrumental
learning (or operant conditioning).

In classical conditioning, a stimulus precedes and elicits a response.
This is the simpler of the two forms of learning. In Pavlov's famous
experiment, a hungry dog who naturally salivated at the sight of food,
but not to the sound of a buzzer, was taught to salivate to the buzzer.
By repeatedly sounding the buzzer prior to presentation of food, the
dog was conditioned to salivate at the sound of the buzzer (Pavlov,
1927). In this type of learning, the food is referred to as an unconditioned
stimulus, salivation to the food as the unconditioned response, the
buzzer is referred to as the conditioned stimulus, and salivation to the
buzzer as the conditioned response. The same demonstration was
made in humans (Watson and Raynor, 1920). A sudden loud noise,
such as a hammer striking a steel bar, was found to elicit fear reactions
from young children. The experimenters also showed that small animals, such as white rats and rabbits, elicited no fear reactions, but
instead reactions of interest and pleasure. In their experiment, after a
number of presentations of these animals together with the loud noise,
the animal came to elicit the fear response from the child. A familiar
example in everyday life is found in the case of a child who is taken to
a doctor's office for the first time to receive an injection. With no prior
experience in the situation the child shows no distress when taken to
the office. However, because the injection is painful, on subsequent
visits the child shows distress (fear) even before the injection occurs.
The doctor has become a conditioned stimulus for fear. Similarly, take
the case of a young woman who receives a rejection letter from her
beloved while she is listening to a favorite piece of music and the music
continues to play while she feels her grief. Years later she may begin
to well up with tears when the same piece of music is played on the
radio while she is driving her car, even though the grief from her loss

is long passed and she has no awareness of the basis for her reaction. Thus, when a previously neutral stimulus is paired with a stimulus that naturally produces a particular response, such that the neutral stimulus comes to elicit the same response, this form of learning is called respondent or classical conditioning.

Extinction

One principle of learning is extinction, which occurs when an unconditioned stimulus is repeatedly omitted (for example, food in the Pavlov experiment and the loud noise in the Watson and Raynor experiment). Under these experimental conditions, the conditioned response gradually diminishes. Extinction, therefore, has to do with a change in the arrangement of the environment, an important principle in addressing the treatment of human disorder, where the goal is to terminate dysfunctional behaviors.

An example of the use of this principle is found in the work of Joseph Wolpe, who devised a treatment for phobias called systematic desensitization (Wolpe, 1958). Until the 1960s, phobias were regarded as largely intractable conditions. Psychoanalytic theory explained phobias as symbolic representations of an underlying conflict. It was claimed that elimination of the phobia required the identification and resolution of the unconscious state from which it arose. Very few patients succeeded in overcoming their phobias with this treatment despite months, even years, of effort in therapy. Wolpe devised a behavioral treatment program that was derived from experiments on cats that had been taught specific fears along the lines of the Watson and Raynor experiment and had then undergone an extinction procedure to eliminate their fear. Systematic desensitization was found to be remarkably effective in removing phobias in a small number of sessions. In systematic desensitization, the patient is taught a technique of relaxation and then gradually exposed to approximations in imagination of the feared object so that the fear response is not elicited. The patient eventually faces the object itself, while in a relaxed state, and the fear response is extinguished.

Generalization and Discrimination

Acquisition of a conditioned response has been shown to lead to that response occurring to similar stimuli. This is called generalization. For example, fears elicited in the child receiving the injection in the doctor's office may generalize to other offices or to other physical characteristics of unfamiliar men who look similar to the doctor, such as men with beards or tall men. This suggests how fears spread in everyday life and how, in the absence of awareness of the learning history of an individual, such fears may be difficult to understand. Psychologists have learned that there are ways to limit generalization. When two stimuli are similar, reinforcement of one (that is, following it with the unconditioned stimulus) and extinction of the other leads to discrimination rather than generalization. Behavior therapists use this principle to eliminate fears and the dysfunctional behaviors prompted by those fears.

Instrumental or Operant Conditioning

The second form of learning, operant conditioning, takes place under different conditions. Here, there is a reversal of the stimulus and the individual's response. The organism first emits a response within a situation, which is followed by some event in the environment that is contingent upon that response. Operant conditioning is determined by its consequences. For example, a hungry dog goes to the bowl where he has been fed, and a child learns to say "please" and "thank you" as a result of parental praise. When favorable consequences occur, the operant behavior is more likely to be repeated in similar circumstances. Whereas respondent conditioning tends to be associated with involuntary musculature, operant conditioning occurs in relation to voluntary musculature. Complex human behavior is formed primarily through operant conditioning. However, psychologists have taken interest in respondent conditioning because of its influence over the physiological condition of behavior, which frequently has important ramifications with respect to emotional reactions.

Reinforcement

Reinforcement is the basic principle of operant behavior. It not only specifies how the frequency of operant behavior is increased, but also specifies the conditioning of reflexes in respondent conditioning. The definition of a reinforcing stimulus is empirical: a stimulus is defined as a reinforcer when it is associated with an alteration in the frequency of a behavior. Food is generally regarded as a primary reinforcer because its visceral effect does not have to be learned. Money and praise are spoken of as conditioned reinforcers because they are established as reinforcers by learning. However, food may be demonstrated empirically to be a reinforcer only when the organism is not satiated. The important point, whether seeking to change "normal" or "abnormal" human behavior, is that a reinforcer for an individual is identifiable only from observing that person's behavior, which has been shaped by his or her unique history.

As we develop from birth, we make random movements, some motor and some vocal. When a stimulus that follows a behavior is associated with an increase in that behavior, it is referred to as a reinforcing stimulus. For a baby, some reinforcing stimuli have to do with reducing deprivation (for example, hunger); others have to do with termination of an unpleasant state (a wet diaper). The former are called positive reinforcers, the latter, negative reinforcers. Behaviors that are followed by termination of a pleasant state or with the onset of an aversive state are likely to decrease in frequency. This, too, has important implications for the understanding of mental disorder and how to change it.

An experiment by Miller (1948) illustrates how this form of learning is particularly relevant to the development of mental disorder. Rats were placed in an apparatus comprised of two compartments, one black and one white, between which there was an open door. Initially, the animals showed no fear of either compartment. The rats were taught to fear the white compartment by the delivering of a mild electric shock through a grid on the compartment's floor. Animals learned to escape the shock by running through the open doorway. On later trials, even though the apparatus to deliver the shock was disconnected, animals placed in the white compartment quickly ran through the doorway to escape from the white compartment. The escape behavior occurred because it was maintained by a decrease in the conditioned fear of the white compartment. When the door was closed, confining the animals to the white compartment, the rats showed strong signs of fear, demonstrating that fear had been learned to the cues in the white compartment. In experiments in which the shock was turned off and the door remained closed, extinction of the fear occurred within a few trials.

In other experiments, a procedure was adopted to determine whether the conditioned fear to the white compartment would motivate the acquisition of a new response that would be reinforced by escaping from the white compartment. With the door closed, when animals in their random agitation happened to press a bar in the white compartment, the door opened, allowing the rats to escape. The rats quickly learned to press the bar. Despite the absence of the electric shock, a response that reduced fear came to reinforce the learning of new behavior. The experiment demonstrated how fears are learned, how they instigate behavior, and how avoidance responses that reduce fear are learned.

Avoidance Behavior

A very important aspect of the Miller experiment and many other experiments such as this one is that the animal's avoidance learning prevented the rat from undergoing extinction (to the absence of the electric shock). One could say that because of learned avoidance behavior the animal failed to learn that conditions had changed and the white compartment was now safe. Conditioned reinforcement in avoidance learning includes internal physiological responses. Aversive stimuli naturally lead to physiological responses in the organism. If an electric shock is administered to an animal, changes occur in its autonomic nervous system, such as an increase in heart rate and more blood delivery to voluntary musculature (necessary for the fight or flight response). Whenever such aversive stimuli are paired with neutral stimuli, they come to function as conditioned negative reinforcers since any response that removes them is negatively reinforced. In humans, these conditioned aversive responses constitute what we refer to as anxiety. Once learned, any stimulus that has acquired negative reinforcement value transfers such an effect to a neutral stimulus occurring contiguously. This feature, too, has important significance clinically.

First described by W. B. Cannon in the 1920s (Cannon, 1929), the fight-or-flight response is our nervous system's reaction to stress by means of hormonal discharges of adrenalin and noradrenalin, followed by the steroid cortisol. This prepares the organism for action by causing the heart to speed up, eyes to dilate, skin to cool (that clammy feeling), and the striated muscles to be readied for maximum movement to contend with the danger. There is no difference between rats and humans in this regard—all animals respond to threat in this way. In humans the fear center in the brain has come to be known as the amygdala, which is an area of the brain located in the anterior portions of the temporal lobes that receives stimuli from various parts of the limbic system and sends signals to other parts of the brain. How this works in controversial, but what is well established is that the fear responses generated are highly subject to learning. Conditioned emotional responses have been studied for years and now how they are created and maintained is well understood. Learned responses to heightened emotion are not only highly prevalent in humans, they characterize mental disorders. This is significant because, as we shall see, it is understanding what people learn to do under the instigation of fear that is crucial to understanding mental disorder. Our behavioral response to these negative feelings, more than the feelings themselves, determines our emotional condition in life. Equally important, studies have made it clear that emotional learning takes place regardless of whether the perceived threat is real or imagined.

These experiments demonstrate how powerful avoidance behavior can be. In humans, many mental disorders are the result of such learned avoidance that maintains highly dysfunctional behavior. In fact, all of the anxiety disorders listed in the *Diagnostic and Statistical Manual of Mental Disorders* (DSM) are illustrations of various ways in which the principle of negative reinforcement has produced different kinds of avoidance behavior that has been cited to characterize these disorders topographically. Take phobias, for example. Let's look at someone who suffers from a phobia about elevators, who has taken a new job on the fifth floor of an office building. Each day he finds himself with a choice of walking up five flights of stairs or confronting his fears by riding in an elevator. After several days of choosing the stairs, he decides that he will take the elevator the next day. Since he is removed in time from doing so, he experiences minimal anxiety. However, the next day, the closer he gets to riding the elevator, the stronger his fears become. While waiting for the elevator he experiences intense anxiety. At that point he thinks, "This is too difficult, I will take the elevator tomorrow," and he walks away to take the stairs. His avoidance behavior is immediately reinforced by his experiencing a very noticeable reduction in his level of anxiety. What is crucial to understanding this disorder is that each avoidance experience is in effect a learning trial that strengthens the disordered behavior as a function of negative reinforcement. Consequently, it is unfortunately the case that it is the behavior of avoidance that maintains the disorder.

Another example is someone who suffers from what is diagnosed as obsessive-compulsive disorder, whose problem is checking. A common form this disorder takes is a fear that the gas stove in the house has not been fully turned off and the house may be filling with gas. The person returns to the stove to check to be certain the gas is fully turned off. When she checks the stove, her anxiety is relieved as a result of negative reinforcement. However, upon walking away from the stove, she thinks, "Did I really turn the knob all the way off?" and the farther she gets from the stove the greater is her anxiety. This leads to the urge to check again, with the same result. People with this disorder can spend hours engaging in this negatively reinforced behavior. Others diagnosed with obsessive-compulsive disorder engage in repetitive hand-washing to the point where their hands become raw. Such a person feels contaminated by having touched ordinary objects (such as door knobs) and washes his hands to free himself of anxiety. Hand-washing, however, while negatively reinforced by anxiety reduction, fails to work because he soon questions whether he did a good enough job or whether he has touched something else that is regarded as dangerous.

The irony of all these cases—whether it is hand-washing, checking, or avoidance of elevators—is that the avoidance behavior that is sought to be the solution to the problem is, in fact, what creates and maintains the disorder. And while these various behavioral manifestations are labeled in the DSM as different diagnostic categories, effective treatment requires an understanding that what characterizes all of them is the functional relationship between what instigates a person's fear and the particular avoidance behaviors that have been learned in response.

Discriminative Stimuli

Another important concept is that of discriminative stimuli. A discriminative stimulus specifies the conditions under which an operant will be emitted because it has reinforcing consequences. A green traffic light is a discriminative stimulus for an operant—for a driver, it elicits pressing one's foot to the accelerator. This is a different reaction from the contraction of one's pupil to a bright light, which is a stimulus that elicits the response as a reflex. Other stimuli, because they are associated with reinforcing stimuli, become reinforcers themselves. Pedestrians learn to press a button at a crosswalk to get a "walk" signal. Reinforcers acquired in this fashion are referred to as acquired or secondary reinforcers. Money, praise, and attention are examples of secondary reinforcers, making it clear that secondary reinforcers exercise powerful control over human behavior, playing a far greater role than primary reinforcers (for example, food) for most people. Psychologists have studied extensively how different schedules of reinforcement affect learning, how behavior may be gradually acquired through reinforcement of successive approximations (shaping), and how behavior can be altered through reinforcement of increasingly longer sets of responses (chaining). All of these techniques go beyond the subject matter of this book but have relevance for the remedying of disordered behavior.

Cognition

In 1977 a very influential paper was published by Albert Bandura which reviewed the theoretical and empirical behavioral literature and gave greater weight to verbal processes in accounting for human behavior. Bandura continued to emphasize the importance of avoidance learning as the prime feature of mental disorder, but the explanation that he offered for what controlled avoidance had to do with cognitive elements: learned beliefs, assumptions, appraisals, and expectations (Bandura, 1977). He hypothesized that expectations having to do with personal efficacy determined how a person would behave in the face of obstacles and aversive experiences. He proposed that psychological methods of treatment were successful to the extent that they altered the level and strength of a person's sense of self-efficacy by determining how much effort will be expended to overcome these situations or whether to avoid them. Bandura defined self-efficacy as a person's subjective estimate of his or her capability to cope effectively with whatever problems arise. He reviewed research on how cognitive processes play a significant role in the acquisition and maintenance of new behavior—for example, how by observing the varying effects of their own actions, people learn what behaviors are appropriate in different settings. He argued that cognitive representations of future outcomes often motivate behavior, and he postulated that behavior was reinforced on the basis of expectations about how certain actions will lead to rewards or avert problems.

This is a different behavioral theory for avoidance behavior. It accords the central role to cognitive experiences. In more traditional behavioral formulations, there is no prerequisite of a cognitive element in the principles outlined. This is not to say that behaviorists with this viewpoint believe that language and cognition are unimportant determinants of human behavior. An abundance of evidence indicates that much of our behavior is under the control of our experience with our environment and requires no cognitive element to guide it. While it is now quite evident that cognitive distortions are significant contributors to mental disorder, including depression, it is also clear that in many ways intellectual processes play a weaker role in human behavior than we would like to believe. Because it is important to us to believe that our actions are rational, in many instances the explanations that we offer to ourselves and others to account for what we are doing and why we are doing it may have little to do with what is actually controlling our behavior. This is clearly true within the parameters of both of the views of reinforcement contingencies just described.

It is not uncommon to account for our behavior as based on our "wanting to" or our "knowing" something, when such explanations may have little or nothing to do with how our behavior was acquired and how it is being maintained. One of the values of therapy is that a therapist has been trained to understand how to study the true basis for behavior and is less likely to be thrown off by the faulty explanations we persuasively give ourselves.

Behaviorists differ over these two conceptions of how to understand the theoretical underpinnings of avoidance behavior. More research is needed to determine how these two concepts of reinforcement account for the complexity of human behavior. A good deal of research on successful behavioral treatment methods is based on principles of reinforcement without appeal to cognitive processes. However, a considerable amount of research has been conducted on the effectiveness of cognitive-behavioral therapy, which has its theoretical base in cognitive theory. Results of both of these behavioral approaches with respect to outcome research are reviewed in Chapter 6.

The Behavioral Model of Functional Relationships

The behavioral model we have outlined having to do with how learning is acquired and maintained, whether that behavior is regarded as "normal" or disordered, is a quite different model from the medical or disease model described in Chapter 1. In the medical model, symptoms of physical disease are produced by an underlying cause such as germs or viruses or lesions. Theorists who adhere to a biological viewpoint of mental disorder adopted this conceptualization in postulating an underlying cause for mental disorder. They view symptoms of mental disorder as manifestations of an underlying disease process, some appealing to physical processes (the predominant theory today), others to psychological processes. Stemming from the medical model, the mentally disordered are called "patients" with a "mental illness." However, as described in Chapter 1, the theoretical formulations of diagnosis in mental disorder and the therapies devised for mental disorder have not been derived from any established underlying cause. And psychotherapeutic practices usually make little distinction from one disorder to another. Diagnoses made from the *Diagnostic and Statistical Manual of Mental Disorders* are based upon topographical descriptions of behavior made in the absence of an adequate empirical underpinning. In fact, the classification of behavior as disordered usually depends upon such things as whether the behavior is disapproved of in a given society;

how unpleasant the behavior is to others; how divergent it is from social norms; and the age, sex, and social background of the individual. The diagnostic label in mental disorder is contextual, whereas the medical model when applied to physical disorder is based upon internal organic pathology, not upon abstractions based upon social values and practices.

An analysis predicated upon an understanding of how behavior is learned makes no claim of an underlying psychological or physical cause for behavior. The model is a functional one that specifies how behavior is acquired and maintained. It is a learning model that is capable of explicitly accounting for behavior. The learning model specifies behavior as a function of learned sequences made up of ante-cedent conditions, the occurrence of a particular behavior, and the consequences that follow the occurrence of that behavior. Thus, in this model behavior is explainable on the basis of its antecedents and its consequences, all of which are observable. There is no appeal in this accounting to an underlying state. The next chapter illustrates how this is applied to case examples of persons suffering from anxiety and depression. It is a model that does not exclude biological factors. There is room within it for specifying variations in temperament, a biologi-cally based state, that produce differences in sensitivity to stimulation. However, while such factors may constitute part of the antecedent conditions in a behavioral sequence, they are not the basic mechanism determining behavior. The point we wish to make is that whatever learned or unlearned setting conditions may be present and elements of the context for a given individual, behavior is explainable according to the tenets specified by the functional model. Hence, you will find references throughout this book to a biopsychosocial model for explaining human behavior, including depression.

"When the actual social learning history of maladaptive behavior is known, the basic principles of learning provide a completely adequate interpretation of many psychopathological phenomena, and explana-tions in terms of symptoms with underlying disorders become super-fluous" (Bandura, 1963).

Classification of Mental Disorder

As discussed in Chapter 2, the *Diagnostic and Statistical Manual of Mental Disorders* provides diagnoses of psychiatric disorders in terms of the form and severity of certain characteristics that are categorized as schizophrenia and other psychotic disorders, mood disorders, anxiety disorders, eating disorders, and so forth. There are 18 of these major categories, 51 subcategories, and 327 different diagnoses. In practice, when mental health practitioners make a diagnosis, they also are expected to rate the severity of the disorder as being mild, moderate, or severe. Secondary diagnoses generally are expected to be made as well. As discussed in Chapter 1, given the ambiguity and overlap of shared characteristics in the descriptions, the level of clinical judgment necessary for making accurate diagnoses reduces the reliability of the manual.

The system is based upon aspects of the persons being diagnosed, not on an interaction between subject variables, learning histories, and stimulus situations. As the foregoing behavioral analysis of the conditions of learning makes clear, a behavioral analysis dictates instead a system based on a social learning paradigm. Psychopathology is to be understood as the learning of dysfunctional behavior according to the same general principles that govern all learning. Learning and behavior take place in a given context, and environmental factors are extremely important. The DSM takes into account psychosocial factors, but they are considered mostly as secondary phenomena that may exacerbate problems or predict prognosis. Clearly, given the unreliability of the DSM, there must be a better way of classifying what is regarded as mentally disordered behavior.

Some years ago, a social learning classification system was proposed that represents a good start as an alternative to the DSM (Staats & Staats, 1963). It is a functional model of different patterns of dysfunctional behavior that are derived from particular learning histories that follow the same principles of learning as that leading to more functional behavior. Each of these conditions requires specific therapeutic remedies closely tied to those histories. The classification includes: behavioral deficits, defective stimulus control of behavior, inappropriate stimulus control of behavior, defective or inappropriate incentive systems, aversive behavioral repertoires, and aversive self-reinforcing systems. Disordered behavior may be describable by one or more of these classifications, depending upon the particular factors that are controlling the behavior specified by each description. The system does not have the jazzy or impressive appearance of the DSM diagnoses, but it has the virtue of promising a lot more utility. Here is synopsis of the system:

Behavioral Deficits

Some disorders reflect an absence of an important coping skill. This deficit may produce problems in social, academic, or vocational situations. A common example is found in people who are avoidant of social situations, causing them to fail to learn good social skills. As a result, they are more likely to experience rejection, reduced income, and to become demoralized. The condition may arise through the absence of good role models in childhood or some set of conditions that led to a failure in reinforcement of effective behavior necessary to deal with life's demands. People diagnosed under DSM as having social phobia or agoraphobia fall in this category; in addition to the disorder being the outcome of avoidance behavior in social situations, a feature of their problem involves absence of a social skill. For such cases, behavior therapists include social skills training as part of the therapy that addresses the avoidance behavior.

Defective Stimulus Control of Behavior

The possession of an adequate repertoire of behavior does not guarantee that a person will respond appropriately. Social situations are complex and require discrimination. Some instances of mental disorder reflect defective stimulus control, which may come about because of poor social training or as a result of a breakdown in discrimination. An experiment by Ayllon and Haughton (1962) explored this condition in a group of psychotic patients with chronic and severe eating disorders who ignored calls to meals. The researchers guessed that the well-intended coaxing of the nurses somehow reinforced the eating problems. A procedure was adopted whereby patients who responded within 30 minutes were fed and all the others were then locked out. Applying this reinforcement contingency to the meal call soon came to govern the behavior of these patients. The time frame was successively adjusted incrementally to 20 minutes, 15 minutes, and finally to 5 minutes. Some people diagnosed as having a personality disorder—such as antisocial personality disorder, borderline personality disorder, and histrionic personality disorder—have histories that quite likely have led to defective stimulus control of their behavior.

Inappropriate Stimulus Control of Behavior

This condition refers to disorders that occur when a previously neutral stimulus inappropriately acquires the capacity to elicit intense emotional reactions. A number of anxiety disorders include somatic complaints of insomnia, agitation, and gastrointestinal distress. Phobias and obsessive-compulsive disorders are clear examples of disorders that arise as a result of aversive respondent conditioning and are maintained by operant avoidance behavior. Behavioral treatments that address this basis for these disorders have been proven to be more effective than any other procedures in treating these conditions.

Defective or Inappropriate Reinforcing Systems

Although most human behavior is acquired and maintained by conditioned positive reinforcers, some mental disorders arise because individuals learn to be reinforced by culturally prohibited stimuli. The diagnoses of paraphilia, exhibitionism, fetishism, pedophilia, and transvestism are examples of disorders with this conditioning background. Once again, the complexity of behavior must be considered, and simple reinforcement paradigms alone probably do not completely account for these behaviors. A sexually maturing boy may experience sexual arousal when touching a silky women's undergarment. Sexual arousal by the feeling of women's garments is reinforced, ultimately, by sexual stimulation and gratification. Wearing women's clothing is reinforced by the sexual excitement involved. This is an example of the cultural context of diagnosis since this is only considered a disorder because of the social sanctions against men wearing women's undergarments. If such behavior were considered acceptable, there would be no need to diagnose or treat transvestism as a condition.

Aversive Behavioral Repertoires

Children who behave aggressively in school as well as a number of the personality disorders listed for adults in the DSM are characterized by behaviors that are aversive to others. It is not unusual to prescribe Ritalin for such children because of behaviors that are unruly, attention-seeking, or aggressive. Treatment agencies for children have high rates of such cases in therapy. As a result of a great deal of research that has been done on aggressive behavior, it is known that responses to stress and frustration generally are learned from observation of adults in similar emotional states. Understanding how the behavior has been learned and how it is being maintained is very important in modifying such aversive behaviors.

Aversive Self-Reinforcing Systems

Because of the importance of verbal behavior and such factors as desire for achievement, individual interpretation of social standards, and personal assessment, self-administered reinforcement comes to play a debilitating role in the lives of some people. Self-evaluation can come under the control of excessively high standards. The mood disorders in the DSM often are characterized by negative self-reflections that give rise to feelings of worthlessness and passivity. Those people whose avoidance behavior has been governed by inappropriate stimulus control and who have aversive self-reinforcing systems are diagnosed with a mood disorder and typically are prescribed antidepressant medication. Many cases diagnosed as substance abuse, most importantly alcohol abuse, fall into this category (Bandura, 1963).

The Need for a Better System

The above taxonomy fully covers the kinds of disordered behavior listed in the DSM but does so by a different system that specifies how the behavior is being controlled by the interactions of that individual with the environment. This system points to specific treatment programs that need to be instituted to extinguish the dysfunctional behavior and teach more functional behavior, a basic principle that is missing in most of the DSM diagnoses. Although it is a system that is in need of further refinement, the taxonomy follows the requirements of science. There may be other systems better than this one, and we would argue that a replacement for the DSM is long overdue. Support of research to develop a taxonomy of this kind has been neglected. The DSM and the International Classification of Diseases are the only diagnostic systems accepted for clinical use. Insurance companies will only reimburse for treatments that are considered "medically necessary." The same faulty reasoning—that if the problem is biological or medical, then it is treatable, but if the cause of a problem is environmental, it is somehow not reimbursable—is used as consistent with the culture of blame referred to previously.

Just because human problems are explained by other factors than biochemical processes and disease entities does not mean that clients seeking psychotherapeutic or behavioral treatment are dealing with mere "quality of life" issues, the treatment of which are not reimbursed by insurance companies. Once again the tail wags the dog, with insurance companies—which must meet a corporate obligation to show profits for shareholders—dictating what constitutes reimbursable care and maintaining reliance on a diagnostic system like the DSM that has theoretical flaws and low reliability. At this point in time, there is very little interest in change because access to quality care would be jeopardized if funding for psychological problems ceased to be reimbursed due to a philosophical position that behavioral health is not "medically necessary." It is time for a more realistic approach to the issues of diagnosis and cost coverage for the treatment of mental disorder that is based in science, not adherence to a dubious status quo.

CHAPTER 5

BEHAVIOR THERAPY

It is often the case when people feel troubled that they have an urge to speak to someone about their problems. Psychotherapists are trained to engage in a particular kind of conversation that is designed to reduce problems brought to them. Many forms of psychotherapy are in use today. They all share the characteristic of being psychological treatments, but there are major differences between them. In addition, the theoretical basis for their treatments varies considerably. Most forms of therapy have as central to their theoretical structure the idea that change comes about mainly through management of the relationship between the therapist and the patient or client. Some treatments are aimed at changing "intrapsychic processes," some seek to provide emotional support, and others use the interpersonal exchange between therapist and client to modify deviant emotional reactions. As discussed earlier, many of the psychotherapies offered today have a theoretical base derived from Freudian theory that regards mental disorder as the product of some underlying psychological process.

Behavior therapy, which is a form of psychotherapy, covers a large number of specific techniques derived from learning theory rather than Freudian psychoanalytic theory and is characterized by some important features that distinguish it from other forms of psychotherapy. Later in this chapter, we describe behavior therapy more fully. It is useful to understand the variety of therapeutic approaches available that comprise the "talking therapies" that are currently used either on their own or with medications. Although it is our belief that the behavior therapies have the strongest scientific support, ultimately treatments need to fit the preferences of the consumers. The main question that remains to be answered in all psychotherapy research is, "Which therapies work, for which clients, and under what conditions?" With the volumes of research into psychotherapy outcomes, and behavioral therapies in particular, therapy matching of technique to client remains an ideal that has not yet been adequately demonstrated.

Classical Psychoanalysis and Psychodynamic Psychotherapy

For most of the last century, the form of psychotherapy that predominated was psychoanalysis and psychoanalytically oriented psychotherapies, which were based upon the classical method, but modified to be briefer and less costly. As briefly described in Chapter 1, Freud's invention, psychoanalysis, was rooted in a theory of the "unconscious." Treatment was aimed at "uncovering" hidden psychological processes, not at eliminating symptoms, which were viewed as defensive reactions that were superficial manifestations of the underlying states. Classical psychoanalysis was focused on treating the "unconscious," which was revealed through the uncovering of repressed childhood conflicts, and accomplished through the gradual resolution of resistance. The treatment was based on an elaborate theory, primarily attributable to Sigmund Freud. It dictated that treatment entailed analyzing the therapist-patient relationship by means of intensive treatment (preferably five sessions per week), making use of the techniques of free association, the analysis of dreams, and a process called "working through of a transference neurosis" (Wolberg, 1967).

Over time, it became clear that there were major problems with psychoanalytic theory and practice. Most importantly, it didn't work very well, or did so only after many years of therapy. Its research base consisted of anecdotal case reports that lacked scientific merit. Psychoanalysis does not measure clinical outcome by symptom change; thus, methodologies for assessing treatment outcome have not easily been applied to the model. When changes do occur, often after many years of treatment, the change may be attributable to the therapy, the passage of time, maturation of the client, and so on. It is difficult to know whether the therapy was responsible for the positive changes. The high cost and limited effectiveness of classical psychoanalysis led to its demise as the primary method of psychotherapy. Psychoanalysis is still practiced today, and it remains intellectually compelling to many therapists and clients. Empirical support for the premise of the theory and treatment is yet to be published, despite many scholarly works on the theory and its application to complex problems.

A number of updated neo-Freudian versions of psychoanalytic theory gradually were devised that have come to dominate the field of psychotherapy. These treatments are less costly, generally entail only one session per week, and the course of therapy is of shorter duration, lasting perhaps a year or two. The name given to these treatments is "psychodynamic psychotherapy." Central Freudian concepts are retained, but they borrow ideas from newer schools of thought on personality development. These treatments continue to emphasize the importance of the relationship between therapist and client as crucial to progress with a primary focus on the importance of early childhood experiences as causing psychological problems.

Psychotherapies differ from one another, depending upon the orientation of the therapist. Psychodynamic psychotherapy, client-centered therapy, and interpersonal psychotherapy represent different schools of thought about how to conduct this process. Typically, regardless of the form of psychotherapy, treatment entails meeting once a week for a number of months, but sometimes for a year or more. The vehicle for success is usually viewed as making particular use of the relationship between the therapist and the patient or client as a means of helping the person better understand his or her personal strengths and weaknesses and to effect changes to improve maladaptive adjustments to life's demands. While this is not true of behavior therapy, it is generally the case that different schools of therapy emphasize the importance of patients achieving "insight" as important to success of treatment. Research has suggested that at least two-thirds of clients in these forms of therapy improve with treatment (Hokanson, 1983). Unfortunately, the research on these approaches continues to be mainly anecdotal, and whatever specific ingredients are important to success remain unknown or unsubstantiated. It is generally understood that there are several common factors in all therapies, including behavior therapy, that have positive impact on the outcome of therapy. These common factors are a good alliance or relationship between the therapist and client, the therapist taking a nonjudgmental stance toward the client and showing positive regard toward the client, and the therapist providing a reasonable rationale for the client's problems and the treatment utilized.

Consumer Reports (1995) magazine conducted a survey of readers who had sought counseling from a mental health specialist. Seligman

(1995) cited this survey as a good example of research on the effectiveness of psychotherapy, although he pointed out its limitations, as have others (Jacobson & Christensen, 1996). Related to our discussion, the survey showed that, according to a self-selected sample of self-reports, 87 percent of people who were feeling "very poor" when they began therapy were feeling better when therapy was finished, and 92 percent of those who were feeling "fairly poorly" at the onset felt better when therapy was completed. According to this survey, longer-term therapy was better than shorter-term, particularly if the duration of therapy was arbitrarily determined by a managed care company or an insurance company's limits on number of sessions. There were no differences between types of therapies employed. This survey gives reason to believe that many people are satisfied with therapy, but it does not meet the rigorous criteria of scientific observation and evaluation that we earlier addressed. A major problem with the survey was that the outcome criteria were vague, and the report does not indicate whether particular treatments reduced specific symptoms or only improved general optimism and social or occupational functioning.

Behavioral psychologists have also stressed the importance of the therapeutic relationship, but with an emphasis on the reinforcement model in the therapy session. For example, Kohlenberg and Tsai (1991) developed functional analytic psychotherapy (FAP) wherein the therapist is alert for clinically relevant behaviors that occur in session. Since many psychotherapy clients experience difficulties in their interpersonal lives, FAP therapists use the therapeutic relationship to elicit clinically relevant behavior, reinforcing those behaviors that will be most functional for the client. A client that lacks assertiveness may say something like "the traffic was terrible today, and I had such a hard time getting here at this time." An FAP therapist might ask, "Are you concerned with the time that we've scheduled our appointment?" to elicit a response from the client that may be a more direct request. If the client says "no," the therapist's hypothesis that the client really wants to change the appointment time is wrong. If the client says "Yes, this isn't a very good time for me," the therapist will reinforce such a direct statement by attending to the request and trying to accommodate a change in scheduling. This is in contrast to the psychoanalytic notion of "working through the transference," wherein the therapist acts as a "blank screen" onto which the client "projects" his or her interpersonal struggles, particularly with parental figures. Behaviorists, even when using the relationship, target behavior and recognize that behavior change occurs as a result of reinforcement or punishment. Cognitive therapists have also emphasized the importance of understanding the client's thoughts and feelings in session (Safran & Segal, 1991). Thus, the stereotype of the cold and clinical cognitive and behavioral therapist is more myth than actuality.

Client-Centered Therapy

In the 1950s, Carl Rogers described a new form of psychotherapy called client-centered therapy (Rogers, 1951). Unlike Freudian theory, which held to a theoretical viewpoint of the nature of mankind as essentially base, Rogers believed in a positive drive for health that had been blocked by negative experiences. He reasoned that since the prime sources of data in psychotherapy were the verbalizations of the client, he took as his subject matter formal characteristics of those verbalizations, specifically looking at the content and emotional loading of statements uttered by the client and how therapists might respond to highlight these elements. His treatment methods were developed through a series of empirical studies he and his students conducted at the University of Chicago Counseling Center. He viewed this study as revealing important elements of what contributed to the strengthening of the therapeutic relationship and that fostered the client's efforts to help him- or herself. Thus, unlike the psychodynamic therapies, Rogers's treatment methods were developed through a series of empirical studies. The primary feature of this new approach was called "active listening." Therapists were trained in the technique of responding to the content and the feeling state implicit in each client statement by paraphrasing. Therapists became skilled through learning a vocabulary of affective words to capture the nature of the utterances. This paraphrasing was seen as a means of facilitating more involvement of the client in the therapeutic process. Objective studies were carried out with college students to assess how this could best be done.

Rogers's method of research constituted an important advance in improving the effectiveness of therapy by insisting upon relying on data to evaluate the theory and the treatment results. Research on active listening made it clear that this approach led to a better understanding by the client as well as the therapist of the nature of the problem presented for treatment. It also provided a methodology for how to explicate the problem and significantly increase client involvement in the process. Moreover, Rogers and his colleagues had devised an approach that demonstrated how to create a strong positive relationship between therapist and client. There is an important sense in which Rogers's work was a forerunner to the development of behavior therapy with his insistence on objective research to describe and evaluate treatment. And his technique made clear how a therapist may construct responses to client verbalizations that convey understanding— a powerful element in the building of the kind of good therapeutic relationship that is important to fostering constructive change. In behavioral terms, Rogers taught therapists how to become positive reinforcers in therapy—qualities deemed important to the building of client confidence and trust.

Behavior Therapy

While behavior therapists regard a therapist's active listening as a necessary ingredient in therapy, they do not view it as sufficient. Behavior therapists now see active listening as one of a number of important therapeutic skills because it aids in creating a helpful relationship and also serves a very useful purpose in eliciting information to properly define the goals of therapy. Behavior therapists also regard insight as neither a necessary nor sufficient condition for treatment, but they do rely on client self-monitoring of behavior to recognize excesses or deficiencies and to track positive changes resulting from the interventions utilized.

At the same time Rogers was doing his work, researchers who had studied the learning process by working with lower animals began looking into applying lessons learned from their research to problematic human behavior. Behavior therapy developed out of this effort and is comprised of a large number of specific techniques aimed at modifying maladaptive human behavior that were derived from these experiments and the theories they spawned. These techniques have included procedures such as systematic desensitization (which is described briefly in Chapter 1), assertiveness training, exposure therapy, cognitive therapy, and behavioral activation. Of particular importance is the work of Lewinsohn, who pointed out the importance of promoting positively reinforced behaviors in addressing depression (Lewinsohn, Biglan, & Zeiss, 1976). Chapter 6 gives a more complete description of the behavioral techniques currently in use to treat depression.

Behavior therapy is based on a number of assumptions (Rimm & Masters, 1974):

1. Relative to psychotherapy, behavior therapy focuses on the maladaptive behavior itself. There is no presumption of an underlying cause.

It does not follow the medical model. Symptoms are viewed as examples of the problem, not as a superficial manifestation of the problem.

2. Behavior therapists assume that the maladaptive behaviors were acquired as a result of the same principles of learning as any other learned behaviors. Excluded, of course, are behaviors that result from a physical trauma, such as physical and mental dysfunctions that arise as a consequence of accidents that have damaged the central nervous system.

3. Behavior therapists assume that psychological principles, particularly principles having to do with the learning process, can be used effectively to reduce maladaptive behavior.

4. Behavior therapists set specific, clearly defined goals in treatment rather than abstract concepts such as "increased maturity" or "personality development." A specific behavior that is presumed to be interfering with the person's functioning is targeted for change. Similar to medicine in which the presenting problem may be "I'm feeling poorly" and the doctor seeks to discover the specific ailments that are giving rise to this report, a behavior therapist seeks to identify behaviors that give rise to a self-description of "My life isn't worth living."

5. Behavior therapists design their treatment to address the particular presenting problem. Most other forms of psychotherapy provide essentially the same approach to all who enter treatment. If a therapist presumes that psychological disorders are the result of an underlying, unconscious process, he or she is not likely to view the presenting problem as what is truly important. A behavior therapist's goal is to remedy the problematic behavior at issue by utilizing different procedures depending upon the nature of the problem. Desensitization may fit one kind of problem, assertiveness training another, skill development another, and so forth.

6. The behavior therapist attends to the here and now. Most other forms of psychotherapy take early childhood experiences as very important and spend a good deal of time discussing those experiences as a means of effecting change. They seek to "uncover" these experiences to gain "insight" as the means of effecting change. Behavior therapists are far more interested in the present, and they don't believe that achieving insight is effective. Behavior therapists believe that the remedy comes from the patient behaving differently in crucial situations. When they do look into experiences that contributed to the learning of maladaptive behavior, they do so in the service of identifying present behaviors to be changed rather than dwelling on the past as particularly helpful in its own right.

7. The techniques of behavior therapy are those that have been subjected to empirical tests and found to be helpful. Behavior therapists

do not assume that a technique is helpful because it is derived from a well-accepted theory, but rather because it has demonstrated effectiveness empirically. This is perhaps the single most definitive feature of behavior therapy in contrast to other forms of psychotherapy.

Cognitive-Behavioral Therapy

A widely practiced branch of behavior therapy is cognitive-behavior therapy. Its basic assumption is that core irrational ideas are at the root of mental disorder. When applied to depression, negative cognitions are assumed to influence the onset and course of depression, and the remedy for the disorder is believed to depend upon a change in these cognitions. Within this framework, what is emphasized is the manner in which humans characteristically process and organize information about experience into belief systems, expectations, and attributions that form the basis for how we interpret what is meaningful in our life. These processes are assumed to be adaptive. Depression, however, is viewed as the outcome of cognitive distortions within this system. It is the outcome of negative beliefs, particularly having to do with a sense of inadequacy, views of others as uncaring, hopelessness about the future, and the conviction of an absence of control over one's life. The goal of cognitive-behavioral therapy is the replacement of these negative perceptions and beliefs with more adaptive ones. Behavioral and cognitive techniques are relied upon to accomplish this goal. Therapists engage in a dialogue with clients with the goal of identifying dysfunctional beliefs and other self-defeating ideas. They assign behavioral experiments to test the validity of beliefs, and behavior therapists assist clients in direct behavior change practices.

Negative Reinforcement and the Avoidance Paradigm

As described in Chapter 1, the first person to successfully make the transition from the laboratory to the consulting room was Joseph Wolpe in the early 1960s. In his treatment for phobias, which he called systematic desensitization, Wolpe taught his patients an anti-anxiety response of muscle relaxation to enable them to experience the feared situation, which was systematically presented in the form of visualized scenes that were arranged in a sequence of increasing difficulty. He thereby provided them with an effective procedure for unlearning their fears.

Wolpe's technique was the first successful application of a method to counteract avoidance behavior, maintained by negative reinforcement, as a means of effecting a cure. While there are a number of different techniques to overcome avoidance behavior, all of the newer behavioral treatments for anxiety conditions that have evolved have identified avoidance behavior as central to the problem. Chapter 4 provides a number of examples of this process, citing phobias and obsessive-compulsive behaviors as illustrations of how the process of negative reinforcement (relief from fear) establishes and maintains the avoidance response.

Effective treatment of these conditions and other mental disorders requires focusing on the choice point such a person faces when confronted by the fear; that is, the point where the process of negative reinforcement, if allowed to occur, will continue to maintain the problem because of avoidance behavior. The therapies that work best are those that provide clients with a way to test and eliminate the fear rather than continue to be controlled by it. These treatments promote taking the risks required to face this choice point constructively by acting rather than avoiding.

It is possible to diagram this process as follows:

A. Elevator phobia:
  1. An experience (actual or modeled) that led the person to learn to fear elevators and avoid them.
  2. Facing an elevator → anxiety ⇒ avoiding taking the elevator → relief from anxiety.
  3. Because what has been reinforced is avoidance behavior, the problem is maintained.

B. Hand-washing:
  1. An experience (perhaps a thought, perhaps a warning from someone significant) that has led this person to develop an excessive fear of illness, disease, or contamination.
  2. Hand-washing is believed to be associated with self-protection against contamination.
  3. Touching a doorknob → anxiety → urge to wash ⇒ hand-washing → anxiety reduction.
  4. Because what has been reinforced is hand-washing, the problem is maintained.

An understanding of the dynamics of these disorders points to the crucial step that maintains the disorder, which is indicated by the double arrows above. This is the point at which behavior occurs that is negatively reinforced. The double arrows may be conceptualized as a choice point, and they are the focus of behavioral treatment. The problem is maintained because the behavior is negatively reinforced. The therapist's task is to explain to the client the nature of this choice point, because effective treatment requires choosing to make a different response at this juncture. As long as the client resorts to the established anxiety-reducing choice, the problem will continue, because while such actions reduce anxiety, the effect is temporary and ensures that the problem will remain. Because it is very difficult to face intense fears without resorting to actions that give immediate relief, it is hard for people to resolve these problems on their own. This is why the skills of a therapist are so important. For therapy to be effective, it usually takes a therapist who has gained trust (this is the sense in which behaviorists also regard the therapeutic relationship as important), who is astute as a diagnostician of behavior (the avoidance paradigms can be complex), and who has the requisite therapeutic skills necessary to help the client to overcome the problem.

Depression

The hallmarks of depression are a shutting down of activity, negative views of oneself, and negative views regarding the future. A major theme to this book is that the typical client diagnosed as depressed has been misdiagnosed and mistreated. This is because there is reason to believe that depression is better conceptualized not as a disease but as a mood state and behavioral state that has developed from the consequences of avoiding anxiety-provoking situations, perhaps including unlearned biological susceptibilities in the form of temperamental factors. Again, this is not a matter of splitting hairs; it is a very different explanation than the one that views depression as a primary condition of biological origin. Effective treatment of depression, just as has been outlined for the anxiety conditions, requires addressing how the avoidance behavior is occurring. Two cases were described in the last chapter that illustrate how this happens: the lonely man who is depressed because he has been unsuccessful dating and the man who becomes depressed as a result of unemployment. We can diagram the role of avoidance leading to depression in these cases as follows:

Case One: The Lonely Man

1. Man goes out on date → has unsuccessful experience → feels disappointment.
2. Repetition of above → absence of relationship with a woman and increasing sense of self as undesirable to women.

3. Man is attracted to a woman and wants to ask her for a date →
   anticipates rejection → experiences anxiety about approaching
   her ⇒ decides against asking her for a date → relief from anxiety.
4. Absence of desirable relationship with a woman and confirmation of
   negative self-views.
5. Depression.

Case Two: Unemployment

1. Man loses his job.
2. Man engages in job-seeking behaviors (calls friends who might
   know of job opportunities, looks at newspaper job listings, contacts
   potential employers to arrange interviews).
3. Repeated experiences of contacting potential employers and going
   for interviews without getting hired.
4. Thinks about continuing job-seeking activities → anticipates rejection
   → anxiety ⇒ stays in bed instead → anxiety reduction.
5. Continuation of unemployment and loss of income, devaluation
   of self.
6. Depression.

Given the circumstances of these cases, it is easy to understand why
the person would be depressed—one needn't invoke any biological
underlying process to explain it. In each of these cases, the double
arrows indicate the points of negative reinforcement leading to avoidance that would be the focus of behavior therapy. The following cases
are more complex examples of how avoidance behavior leads to the
prime features of depression—that is, shutting down of activity, negative
self-views, and hopelessness.

Case Three: Underachievement

A 35-year-old single man came to therapy stating that he felt
depressed. His history reflected underachievement, dependency, social
anxiety, and low self-esteem. Despite being of superior intelligence, he
had had little advancement on his job with an accounting firm, felt
insecure and inadequate, and described a history of bouts with depression. Socially isolated and having few friends, he saw himself as of little
interest to others, particularly women. He also was hypochondriacal,
periodically believing he had contracted some awful disease or that his
body was failing. He wished for years for a better assignment at work
that would be more interesting and offer opportunities for promotion,

but failed to act on it. His family history is one of having been overpro-
tected, frequently being warned by his parents of the dangers lurking
in life.

This case can be diagrammed as follows:

1. As a child, expressing the intention to take independent action →
   warnings by parents of the danger of doing so, including overtaxing
   himself → cancellation of intention.
2. Many repetitions of above in a variety of contexts.
3. As an adult, experiencing the desire to take independent action →
   anxiety regarding the danger of doing so ⇒ cancellation of intention.
4. Development of feelings of insecurity and a self-definition of inadequacy that served to further dissuade him from taking independent
   action.
5. Periodic depression tied to his disappointment in himself as a weak
   and inadequate person.

The depression in this case was the result of fears of asserting himself, which had prevented him from acting on his wishes. His avoidance behavior prevented him from realizing his potential, cutting him
off from the rewards that would follow from asserting himself appropriately. Denied the success he observed in others who were no more
capable than he was and viewing himself as unusually vulnerable, why
wouldn't he feel depressed? Accordingly, therapy was focused on the
importance of his taking initiative despite his fear, providing him with
techniques for controlling his fear about doing so, and helping him to
learn good assertive behavior to enhance the likelihood that taking
action would be successful. Coming to a better sense of himself as
worthwhile and possessing strength required demonstrating to himself, by virtue of his own actions, that he was an adequate, not inadequate, person. Therapy was not directed at his feelings of depression
per se but at avoidance behaviors that gave rise to his feeling
depressed.

Case Four: Selflessness

This is a case of a 30-year-old married woman with no children,
who had experienced success in therapy for depression previously, but
reported that while her life clearly was better in many ways, she periodically fell into a depression that she thought required medication.
She had concluded that because of her biology she was faced with the
inevitability of being periodically depressed. She grew up in a home
with parents who were unhappily married. Her mother regularly

turned to her for solace, lavishly praising her for her devotion when she complied, accusing her of being selfish if she resisted her mother's demands. In effect, her mother trained her to be her caretaker. She became a "good girl" whose main task in life was to take care of her mother and never give her mother any reason to be concerned about her. She was a high achiever in school and developed a keen sense of how to anticipate and fulfill the needs of others. As an adult, she became a social worker, took on the most difficult cases, and devoted herself to the care of others. Periodically, however, she found herself in a "deep depression" that would last for weeks or even months, leading her to return to psychotherapy and take antidepressant medication in an effort to feel better.

This case can be diagrammed as follows:

1. Mother calls for help → child complies → mother rewards her with praise; mother calls for help → child resists → mother labels her selfish.
2. Repetitions of above.
3. Mother calls for help → child prefers to do something else and wishes to refuse → child feels anxious, guilty, selfish ⇒ child complies with mother's demands → mother praises child, shows love for child.
4. Others call for help → child, and later as an adult, prefers to do something else and considers refusing → feelings of anxiety, guilt, and selfishness ⇒ compliance with others' demands → feels good about self.
5. A pattern of relentless selfless behavior is established based upon guilt and a sense of being selfish if she thinks of considering herself.
6. Periodic depression.

Therapy in this case was directed at helping the woman abandon a way of life that was unsustainable because of the self-neglect it entailed. While there were satisfactions in serving others, her inability to attend to herself eventually would lead to depression. How many of us wouldn't be depressed by a life that allowed no attention to our own desires? The situation was akin to what is seen in research studies with lower animals that is referred to as "ratio strain" (Ferster & Perrot, 1968) where too much behavior is required of an animal for it to earn a reward, and which eventually leads to a breakdown in behavior. This woman was trapped in a situation where her conscience dictated constantly being of service to others with little life of her own beyond the satisfactions of self-sacrifice. She could manage it well for periods of time, but periodically she ran out of steam and broke down with awful feelings of depression. This, too, should be understood as a case where the depression was induced by avoidance behavior—avoidance of self-accusations of selfishness she had learned at her mother's knee. The therapeutic solution required that she come to an understanding of the basis for her problem, engage in therapeutic exercises to free her of her feelings of selfishness for wanting to meet her own needs, and develop a better sense of balance so that she met her own needs as well as fulfilled her wishes to be of help to others.

Case Five: Fear of Failure

This is a case of a 50-year-old man, separated from his wife, who has been reasonably successful as a writer with a large company, but had great difficulty completing assignments until faced with an ultimatum to finish his work or lose his job. As a child, he was regarded as gifted. Both of his parents were very successful and they had high expectations of him. He was a high achiever whose studies came very easily and required little effort on his part. His writing and his other intellectual skills were praised by everyone. It was a foregone conclusion that he would excel at whatever he chose to do in life. Later, however, he found that as the intellectual demands increased, more effort was required for success and he came to question just how capable he really was. As an adult, he had achieved some success, but he secretly questioned whether he was the star others thought he was. He often found himself anxious and depressed about whether he could meet the lofty expectations he now carried for himself, which he assumed to be necessary to maintain his image with others. He began to procrastinate, putting off turning in work that he believed failed to meet these high standards. His situation deteriorated when he began turning to alcohol. He finally consulted a psychiatrist who diagnosed the condition as one of an underlying depression, recommending Prozac. Recognizing his dependency on alcohol, the patient was reluctant to turn to a different drug and sought another form of help. He reported feelings of helplessness in overcoming his procrastination and was demoralized and depressed, seeing no way out, even considering ending his life.

This case can be diagrammed as follows:

1. A work product is required → perfectionistic expectations are elicited because of his early history of great success → fear of failure ⇒ avoidance of the task by choosing to do something else → temporary relief from anxiety.

2. Repetition of above.
3. Sense of himself as a fraud who is unable to live up to his own or others' expectations of him.
4. Depression.

Once again, effective therapy is not directed at the feelings of depression, but at helping the man develop more reasonable self-expectations and to learn to meet deadlines. Fear of failure had led to avoidance of productive work, and this avoidance behavior became the focus of therapy. Cognitive therapy aimed at reducing excessively high standards was employed and behavioral techniques were devised, such as devising a graded series of homework assignments designed to teach completing tasks on time.

The point we wish to make is that in each of these cases, the idea of altering biology as a means of effecting a cure is an ill-advised choice of treatment, because it fails to address the trigger of the problem that needs to be modified if the person is to receive the help needed.

College Students

Colleges and universities have intellectual and social environments that are prime conditions for playing out the paradigm just described to account for depression. In our competitive society college campuses have been lively, stimulating places for learning and personal growth, while at the same time environments of high stress, populated by students facing intellectual and emotional challenges that often lead to high anxiety and avoidance behavior. In fact, there is probably no arena that more vividly illustrates the operation of avoidance behavior and its relationship to anxiety and depression than college campuses. College students are in a situation that is characterized by continuous evaluation—a highly anxiety-provoking condition. Students are constantly facing deadlines carrying the risk of devaluation and failure. The success of their performance carries great significance for them in the present and for their future. Under the pressure of such continuous demands that can generate quite frequently occurring anxiety, college students are ripe for avoidance behavior. Procrastination is one of the most common problems faced by college students and is a clear example of avoidance behavior.

The challenges to college students concerning academic success are exacerbated by other issues they face at this time in their lives. For many of them, this is their first time away from home. They are at a time in their lives when their self-concepts are not fully formed, making them more susceptible to self-doubt and self-negation. The situation is complicated by the fact that although they are now young adults they usually remain financially and—to an important extent— emotionally dependent on their parents. They are in a period in their lives that involves a leap toward emancipation from parental control toward greater autonomy, and a time when they are learning to identify themselves as independent adults with the responsibility of choosing lifelong goals on their own terms. Nevertheless, this is a process, and it remains important to them to achieve success not only for themselves, but as proof of their self-worth to parents paying the sizable bills enabling them to go to college. They want their parents to be proud of them. Their parents, for their part, still feel responsible for them, worry about them, and feel a direct stake in their children's success. As a result, parents, while often lending important emotional as well as financial support, sometimes communicate in ways that contribute to the anxiety of their children. In addition, parents engage in well-meaning efforts to arrange help for their children when they report their distress and sometimes these efforts are misguided due to their misunderstanding of the nature of anxiety and depression.

There is some reason to question whether college students are being properly diagnosed and treated. For example, a survey by the American College Health Association of more than 29,000 students found that 7 percent of males and 14 percent of females had been diagnosed as depressed and that 28 percent of males and 38 percent of females were currently taking antidepressant medication (Kadison & DiGeronimo, 2004). A recently published book on the mental health of college students cites a survey of the use of prescription drugs by college students. The most frequently prescribed drug for college students is not the birth control pill, but Prozac. Anxiety agents are second, and in third place are all other antidepressant drugs (Kadison & DiGeronimo, 2004). We believe there is considerable reason to question whether this extent of prescription drug use to treat depression is justified.

The background for these problems faced by college students is easily understood. For many years a college degree has been viewed with some validity as being crucial to success in later life. Performance on examinations determines that outcome and provides regular instances for the management of anxiety. These are exactly the conditions that give rise to depression: avoidance behavior leading to negative outcomes, including negative cognitive and emotional consequences. Because the college years also include requirements for managing challenging new issues with respect to autonomy and social situations, there are other sources of considerable anxiety with opportunities to elect avoidance. For example, negotiating independence from parents is often difficult and complicated, it is not unusual to have to deal with a difficult roommate, there are decisions to be made about the use of alcohol and drugs in the midst of peer pressure, there are questions concerning sexuality, and there are a host of issues related to decision making and problem solving that take on far greater importance. Because of the antianxiety effects of alcohol and some recreational drugs, use of these substances can take on particular importance in this context. All of these issues also give rise to increases in anxiety, may lead to avoidance behavior, and can lead to depression. We believe that the behavioral analysis we have described in this chapter represents a clear-cut explication of how to understand the nature of the problem and, as Chapter 6 will detail, provides a basis for a better method for addressing the problem.

Manifestations

The depressive effects of avoidance behavior are manifested in two ways. The first type of manifestation (let's call it Type A) occurs as a consequence of some alteration in a person's life situation that results in a disruption of that person's previously quite functional ongoing behavior. Typical examples are depressions that occur after the death of a loved one or the loss of income and status following a job loss. In these instances, the person has been cut off from positively reinforcing activities because of the loss and has not found a way of replacing them. Life is no longer happy, and there is no sense of the possibility of a happy future. These are simpler conditions to diagnose and to treat because the cause of the problem is obvious and because what is called for is the reinstatement of previously learned behaviors that are already present in the person's repertoire but are not being expressed. Behavioral activation aims to promote lost behaviors that had been sources of positive reinforcement. For example, in the case of a widow or widower, this often requires the instigation of social behavior. It is not unusual after a period of mourning for such social behavior to be blocked by fears of failure (for example, the idea that the person no longer is attractive) or guilt (stemming from feelings of disloyalty to the deceased partner), negative emotions that set up the avoidance paradigm that interferes with the steps desired for regaining a happy life. Following a job loss, fear of rejection may set in motion a similar process that interferes with job-seeking actions, leading to the sacrifice of problem-solving behaviors that had previously been successfully in place.

The second kind of life situations that give rise to depression, Type B manifestations, are more complex and numerous. They are found in conditions where avoidance behavior is part of the person's characteristic way of life, compromising desired goals and gradually producing consequences that lead to depression. Most of the cases cited above are Type B manifestations. People who suffer from social anxiety, who fail as a result to learn successful social behavior or who fail to achieve their vocational aspirations and eventually become depressed are examples of this Type B manifestation of depression. Because there is no defining event—such as a death or a job loss—that is a readily recognizable precipitant of the depression, more information is necessary to the conduct of therapy to identify the avoidance pattern. Establishing the basis for the depression generally takes longer, but ordinarily a few therapy sessions suffice for the diagnostic process to discover the pattern. In addition, because there generally is a deficit in the person's functioning that has resulted from the avoidance, therapy must be directed toward correcting that deficit. Rather than reinstating behavior that had been ongoing, as in Type A manifestations, the therapy is aimed at teaching the person how to cope with the specific anxiety-provoking situations that have been avoided. For these reasons, therapy for Type B manifestations usually takes longer. Again, behavioral activation is a treatment for depression that is predicated on replacing avoidance behaviors with successful coping behaviors.

The Functional or Learning Model

To reiterate, the theoretical model on which these case analyses are based is not the medical or disease model, but a functional model. Whereas the medical model specifies disorder as the result of some underlying and often hidden cause, the functional model views disorder as controlled by learned sequences of behavior, with the important elements open to observation. What is important in a functional model is the relationship between a behavior, its immediate antecedents, and its immediate consequences.

The problem to be addressed in therapy is conceptualized as changing a particular behavior occurring under particular circumstances—most importantly, avoidance behavior. The significant antecedents to this behavior are comprised of a complex of intentions and emotions within which a particular constructive response has come through learning to stimulate a negative emotional reaction. As a result, this context sets the occasion for that person to emit a different response, an avoidance response. The immediate consequence of the avoidance behavior is a reduction in the aversive emotional state (anxiety), which results in the avoidance behavior coming to predominate. Simply put, to reduce the fear, the person avoids. As outlined in Chapter 4, the mechanism controlling this process is the principle of negative reinforcement. The avoidance behavior produces mental disorder because, while the immediate effect of avoidance is reinforcing, the long-term consequences of avoidance are dysfunctional.

The entire explanation in this model rests on the relationship that exists within a current sequence of experiences and behaviors. Knowing the history of how this sequence was learned can be helpful in defining the problem and may be of intellectual interest, but it is of no pragmatic value in itself. Although a thorough understanding of the learning history or "insight" might be nice, this model indicates that the only satisfactory remedy is one that rests on changing the person's behavior in a specific context. Thus, while the early steps given in the cases described above make reference to a learning history that bears a similarity to the medical model, these steps are not particularly important to the outcome of treatment. The treatment doesn't depend upon the client understanding his or her history. Although helpful in giving the client a basis for understanding how his or her problem may have come about and why the treatment approach makes sense, there is no implication that having "insight" into these factors is necessary or useful as a remedy. Because we have been so inculcated in the medical model, it often helps to provide an explanation of this kind as a bridge to acceptance of this different model. It is an aspect to treatment that also has value as part of a process of relationship-building that will be important when the client faces the very difficult task of challenging his or her fears and needs to trust the therapist to get through it.

The essential line in each of these case analyses that defines the model is the step that has the double arrow, which specifies the behavioral sequence that is maintaining the problem. It is the road map to therapeutic change because it points to what is the real work of therapy—unlearning the functional relationship that supports avoidance behavior that is the cause of the client's misery and replacing it with more constructive behavior.

Behaviorists differ on some aspects of this presentation because one element in the sequence outlined is not observable—that is, the negative emotional reactions (for example, anxiety, guilt) that are hypothesized to be the basis for negative reinforcement. This is a hypothetical construct that is perfectly legitimate in science as long as the construct leads to clear-cut predictions that can be tested. Nevertheless, some behaviorists see this construct as unnecessary and prefer to explain the sequence purely in terms of what is observable. Their treatment procedures are likely to be identical because the paradigm still has avoidance behavior as its primary focus and entails identifying the situations that are the antecedents for these behaviors, as well as setting the goal of arranging a program that leads to the substitution of more constructive behaviors in place of the avoidance.

CHAPTER 6

BEHAVIORAL ANALYSIS, BEHAVIOR THERAPY, AND OUTCOME RESEARCH

Explaining and treating depression has utilized the time and resources of mental health professionals for decades. What was once referred to as "melancholia" is now commonly known as "major depressive disorder," but helping people who are feeling blue, sad, lethargic, and hopeless has long been a goal. Behavior therapists initially focused their treatments on very specific problems such as phobias rather than depression, because depression posed a rather vague set of complaints.

Ferster (1973) proposed the first analysis of depression from a behavioral perspective. According to Ferster, reinforcement schedules and environmental influences were important factors in depressive behavior. He particularly focused on the ways in which escape and avoidance behaviors were reinforced. Ferster was the first to present a behavioral analysis of the phenomenon known as depression, opening the door for other researchers to develop specifically behavioral techniques for treatment.

During the time of Ferster's writing, few practicing psychotherapists paid attention to behavioral concepts such as reinforcement. The prevailing view of depression at the time was a psychoanalytic notion that depression was anger turned inward toward the self. Furthermore, there was an emphasis on early childhood development and psychological disorders. Ferster also looked to early childhood for explanations of depression, but he looked at the possible learning histories and reinforcement processes that might provide an explanation.

Learning begins at birth. Behaviors either increase because they are reinforced or they decrease because they are punished or fail to be reinforced. When an infant cries in response to hunger pangs and is fed, the crying behavior has been positively reinforced. The infant will be more likely to cry the next time she feels the hunger pangs, thus making it more likely that there will be the positive reinforcement of food.

Earliest communication begins in this way. In situations such as the one described above, infants learn that they can have an impact on the environment, and they learn to manipulate the contingencies in the environment to get what is needed. In other instances, if an infant cries and is inconsistently responded to by the parent, crying may increase but not because it was positively reinforced. Instead, crying itself may alleviate some of the distress from the hunger pangs. It is not unusual for infants and young children to cry themselves to sleep, suggesting that crying itself may have a soothing function as well as serving as a means of communication. The relief from distress is a negative reinforcer. Crying gets louder when the infant is on an extinction schedule, but the infant is also responding to her sense of deprivation by crying. The crying continues because it is negatively reinforced, but the infant is not learning to manipulate her environment to get her needs met. She is learning, at a very early age, to be passive and to soothe herself in the absence of getting positive reinforcement from the environment consistently.

In some instances, when getting the reinforcement requires an inordinate amount of responses, the outcome is to give up. This might happen to a toddler who is trying to put pegs in holes on a pegboard. If the child cannot figure out how to place the right shapes into the pegboard, his attempts are not reinforced. He may bang at the toy, but he no longer attempts to place the pegs in the proper holes because the task has required too many responses prior to the reinforcement. The behavior that is likely to increase is banging the toy if there is some pleasure attained from doing so, because banging is the behavior that is reinforced. If the child banged on the toy and the toy was swiftly taken away, the banging behavior would be likely to decrease in the future because it had been punished by the removal of the pegboard.

According to Ferster, when attaining reinforcement requires high levels of response for minimal reward, behaviors that are responses to deprivation will increase. These responses to an internal sense of need or desire may only randomly secure a reward from the environment. This is how depressive behavior works.

Some Examples of the Etiology of Depression

A young man is sad because his beloved has rejected him. When he calls, there is no answer. His letters and emails are not returned. In other words, his behavior is not being reinforced positively in the environment. He may begin to write poetry to his beloved or carry on conversations in his head about what he should have said differently. He is responding to his sense of deprivation. He ruminates about the breakup and spends much of his time moping and brooding. This internal monologue allows a sense of relief, but it also functions like "magical thinking"; if he thinks about it enough, the beloved he yearns for is still present in his life, even though the thoughts are also painful. As he broods, he withdraws from friends and family. He finds it difficult to concentrate at work. He may have thoughts of escaping the emotional pain by committing suicide. If he were to see a mental health professional, he would be given a diagnosis of depression.

Behaviors also decrease when they are punished. If a young girl tries to join a group of children playing kickball and is teased and called names, she is less likely to make future attempts to join the game. If repeated attempts to join groups are punished, she is likely to isolate herself, and she may become shy and socially anxious in group situations. Her feelings of anxiety will prevent her from approaching groups of children, and she will respond to feelings of loneliness through other means than seeking to join a social group. She may develop a friendship one on one with another child, provided those interactions are not punished as well. Or she may spend more time with adults and avoid playing with other children. She may even develop imaginary friends and play by herself in her home, not developing the confidence or skill to engage in age-appropriate social behavior. As she becomes an adolescent or a young adult, her isolation and solitary behavior may make others consider her to be depressed. She may feel badly about herself and develop negative attitudes about herself and others that would cause her to feel sad and lonely.

Recalling the psychoanalytic notion that depression was anger turned inward against the self, Ferster (1973) sought to explain the negative ruminations associated with depression as well as the withdrawal and avoidance behaviors. An example of a small child illustrates the process that Ferster described. When a small child becomes angry with a parent and pokes out his tongue, spits, and says "you're a doo doo head!" he may be punished by being put in a time-out or given a swat in the pants. The parent has punished the *expression* of anger, and spitting and calling someone a "doo doo head" may decrease after repeated attempts are met with similar punishments, but the *feelings* of anger will continue to be present. In the future, when the child becomes angry with a parent, in order to avoid the punishment, he will correct himself first. If the parents have said "you are a very bad boy!" in response to his spitting, he might say to himself "bad boy!" and either take out aggression on a toy or go away to his room to console himself. Telling himself "bad boy!" avoids the punishment but still expresses his feelings. These negative statements may become "self-statements" that are reinforced by the avoidance of painful consequences from the environment. An adult who enters the wrong room while an important meeting is going on and feels embarrassed says to herself as she quickly closes the door behind her, "How stupid of me." She is behaving in a similar manner, and her negative self-statement is reinforced if it provides any relief from her feelings of embarrassment.

There are many varying schedules of reinforcement that produce different rates of behavior and varying resistance to extinction. Behaviors increase or decrease based on the principles of operant conditioning as well as those of classical conditioning. Many emotions are classically conditioned responses to certain environmental factors or to private events, such as the words that stream through our brains in the form of thinking. Consider the reaction you might have if, shortly after the loss of a loved one, you heard his or her name while you're attending a small gathering of friends. The sound of the name will elicit an immediate reaction from you. It may be a feeling in the pit of your stomach, a wave of sadness, an urge to cry, or simply a need to turn your head in the direction of the person speaking the name. The name of your loved one has been paired with intense feelings of distress or longing, and simply hearing the name, even if the speaker was not referring to your loved one, but to someone with the same name, will occasion a reaction.

Unrealistic Ideas and Depression

Melancholy has been identified as a problem since the days of Hippocrates, yet we only understand dysphoric moods to be problematic in comparison to cultural standards of emotional regulation. In Western culture, people tend to seek equilibrium in their lives. In diagnosing depression or other disorders, mental health professionals tacitly endorse an idea that there is some ideal level of emotional reactivity.

One is expected to be exuberant on a special day like a wedding day, graduation from college, or at the birth of one's child, but such exuberance is considered maladaptive while shopping for groceries. If people really reacted to such basic necessities as a new pair of jeans or a soft drink in the fashion depicted in television commercials, those people would very likely be considered manic by most standards. Likewise, it is acceptable to be withdrawn, tearful, and lethargic following the death of a loved one, but when this state occurs in the absence of such a loss, or lasts too long by community standards, a diagnosis of depression is made. It is possible that part of the suffering experienced by depressed or anxious people is due to the recognition that they are outside the norm. In a sense, the depressed person may ask, "why is everyone else happy and I am so miserable?" Reactions of this kind are not uncommon around holidays, when there is a cultural expectation of happiness. The person has fallen short of the ideal that is expected. Unfortunately, because of media depictions of beautiful people dancing on sunny boat docks because of the beer they are imbibing or the frock they are wearing, some people expect that there is a level of exuberant happiness that they are missing out on. The suffering becomes worse in the comparison to an unrealistic depiction of enthusiastic people reacting with great joy to a new version of a breakfast cereal.

Throughout this book we have been examining the two conflicting theories to account for depression—the biological theory and the behavioral theory. From a biological viewpoint, depression is seen as a disease entity with an underlying physical basis. Aside from the problem that the diagnosis of depression is far from reliable, there are other problems with this conceptualization: (1) There are no homogeneous symptoms of depression, (2) there is an implied discontinuity between "normal" mood states of sadness and "abnormal" mood states of depression, and (3) such a viewpoint ignores how the person's life situation is related to depression. It may be true that people become sad, lethargic, and withdrawn following a loss, and medication may alleviate some of these symptoms, but few reasonable physicians would prescribe medication to take away the normal experience of grief. However, when the feelings have continued for too long, based on either a cultural expectation that a person should have moved forward or the person's distress over feeling distress, medication would typically be suggested. The implication is that an illness has developed, ignoring the multiple ways that people experience life based on their reinforcement histories and developmental experiences. These are some of the reasons behaviorists take issue with the biological explanation.

From a behavioral standpoint, depression is the outcome of behaviors governed by unfavorable reinforcement contingencies. Depression reflects insufficient positive reinforcement for adaptive activities, with reinforcement occurring instead for behaviors that are maladaptive. The discussion in Chapter 4 of the power of the immediate consequences of behavior over long-term consequences is most relevant in this regard. As we have seen, other behavioral theorists point to the importance of cognitive factors controlling this state. A number of behavioral theorists have offered conceptualizations about how depression develops.

Reinforcement Models

Two theorists have extended Ferster's ideas—Lewinsohn and Seligman. Lewinsohn (1974) theorized that depression results from a low rate of response-contingent positive reinforcement. It is learned. The causes are attributed to a reduction in pleasurable activities or through loss. He pointed to several causative sources: an environment that provided too little positive reinforcement, poor social skills so that the person's behavior elicits too little in the way of positive reinforcement from others, or the presence of anxiety that blocks the individual's appreciation of reinforcers that are present. He described the process as one that may be subtle or slow, or it may be readily identifiable as the result of the loss of an important reinforcer, such as the death of a loved one or loss of a job. Depression is regarded as occurring when the net gain associated with responding adaptively is lower than the gains from inactivity. The resultant cognitive features of inactivity, reduced self-esteem, helplessness, and hopelessness are what characterize depression. Furthermore, he believed that depressive behavior is maintained most importantly by its reinforcement contingencies, but Lewinsohn also discussed how the elicited attention and sympathy sometimes become substitutes for the lost positive reinforcement.

Seligman (1975) offered the view that depression occurs when there is a lack of contingency between a person's behavior and important life events. He called this effect "learned helplessness." His formulation was derived from experiments he had done with animals. Dogs that were unable to escape from shock had been found to develop learning problems and emotional deficits (Seligman & Maier, 1967). He postulated that the helplessness/hopelessness characteristic of depression comes about as the result of experiences that lead to an expectation of an inability to have any control over important outcomes in one's life.

Social Skills Models

In addition to Lewinsohn, who suggested that social skills deficits were one of the factors causing depression, a number of other behavioral theorists and researchers have pointed to deficiencies in problem-solving skills as factors in the development of depression. Wolpe (1979) regarded social skills deficits attributable to anxiety as important determinants of depression, and others have described skills deficits in marriage as responsible for depression (Beach & O'Leary, 1986; Jacobson, Holtzworth-Munroe, & Schmaling, 1989). Lewinsohn provided research evidence for this proposition (Lewinsohn, Mischell, Chaplin, & Barton, 1980).

Cognitive Theory

Seligman's learned helplessness theory is a cognitive theory in that it is rooted in an assumption about one's futility to affect important future events. The cognitive theories of depression that have been most influential have been those of Ellis (1962) and Beck (Beck, Rush, Shaw, & Emery, 1979). Cognitive theories conceptualize depression as the result of the development of faulty perceptions and appraisals of events. Negative cognitions in the form of negative attitudes and negative self-statements arise as the result of adopting negative beliefs that shape how views of the self, the world, and the future are organized. Beck refers to this as the "negative triad" (Beck, 1967). The cognitive features of low self-esteem, self-blame, a sense of deprivation, and feelings of being overwhelmed by responsibilities are derived from negative interpretations of events in the lives of people who develop depression. Beck's theory also posits that individual differences in the reinforcement value associated with different kinds of life experiences are responsible for activating cognitive vulnerabilities for depression. Individuals for whom self-worth is tied more to social relationships are high in "sociotropy" and are particularly vulnerable to social losses; those for whom independence and achievement are more highly reinforcing—that is, high in "autonomy"—are more vulnerable to the experience of failure or threats to their control.

Integration

There is an old story of the three blind men who come upon an elephant for the first time. One of the men is at the elephant's head, another at the animal's side, and the third at the elephant's tail. Each describes the elephant according to his observations gained from touch. The one at the head defines the elephant in terms of its long, muscular, flexible trunk. The one at the elephant's side sees the elephant in terms of its wide expanse of tough, loose, leathery skin. The man at the elephant's rear conceives of the elephant in terms of its pillar-like legs and tiny tail. Each has truthful information, yet what they are describing, based on their limited knowledge, is a quite different description of an elephant. To the extent that they independently extrapolate from their observations, one can expect a good deal of error about inferences they make that go beyond what they have learned from their own hands. This is a good metaphor for the state of affairs with respect to behavioral theories of depression.

A background of solid research provides a context. There have been lines of research with theoretical models based on the results of controlled experiments of those models. All of the behavioral theories summarized here are probably part of the truth about depression. However, it is likely that there is error in these conceptualizations as well, and it is clear that a lot more research is needed before the full picture of depression is understood. In the meantime, there is good reason to believe, based on the results of a host of experiments done in the behavioral frameworks described above, that reinforcement principles are basic to the problem, that cognitive elements are very important to an understanding of how the depression is expressed, and that addressing avoidance behavior is central to the remedy.

The hallmark of the behavioral theory we are presenting is based on avoidance behavior being the prime mechanism in the learning of negative cognitions. Depression is the outcome of the combination of these two behavioral processes, both of which maintain the negative system basic to depression. In order for depression to be remedied, the negative cognitions must be corrected, and in order for this correction to occur, avoidance behavior ultimately must be replaced by more adaptive behavior. Success in therapy, therefore, usually requires not only addressing the irrational negative ideas but, more importantly, the avoidance behavior that sustains those ideas.

By now it will not escape the reader's attention that, like the biological explanation, a behavioral or psychological explanation for depression possibly describes only "one side of the elephant." Certainly, both fields of inquiry have valid justifications for continuing their search to find suitable methods for helping people mitigate the sufferings of life. The professions of psychiatry, psychology, and other mental health disciplines are in danger of jumping to conclusions too rapidly based on their research. This is why there are criteria for understanding the significance, ability to generalize, and need for replication of findings. People function as a complex whole, not as biochemical automatons or rats in a behavioral experiment. Although recent research suggests that distinct brain activity differentiates groups of depressed people as observed by positron emission tomography (PET) scans (Seminowicz et al., 2004), and such research may lead to a better understanding of differential treatments, these data do not support the wholesale use of antidepressant medication for depressed people, nor do they necessarily imply a biological basis for depression. Keep in mind that PET scans show varying glucose levels and other changes in the brain when a person thinks about various topics—for example, ruminating on one's own funeral service or imagining having a sexual encounter with a highly desirable partner. Life experiences have been found to affect brain chemistry, so it is not clear under what circumstances one process is more basic to the other. It is also true that behavioral and cognitive-behavioral therapies have been shown to influence both environmental and biological elements of depression (Goldapple et al., 2004).

All of these behavioral approaches focus far more on the present rather than on the past in applying their theoretical orientations to therapy. With so many classically and operantly conditioned responses, it is impossible to figure out what historical events in our lives have caused any current feelings or behaviors. For this reason, behavior therapy and cognitive-behavior therapy, while examining the past to help formulate a statement of the problem, focus on the here and now, using the opportunities that we now have to evaluate the function of our behaviors and thoughts so that we can make changes that are likely to help in the future. Understanding why you are this way or that may be interesting, but it is imprecise and does not necessarily lead to change that will make your life better in the future. Moreover, whatever factors were important in establishing and maintaining the behavior are operating in the present and are open to observation.

Behavior Therapy

Exactly what is meant by behavior therapy? Behavior therapy is defined as the application of experimentally derived principles to modify human behavior that has been classified as deviant. It is a collection of specific techniques, for the most part derived from learning principles, that are applied to effect behavioral and emotional change within the context of a social situation comprised of a therapist and a client. It is not simply a collection of procedures, but an integrated treatment methodology under an umbrella theoretical framework. And whereas psychodynamic therapists see the therapeutic relationship as central to the therapy (as an extension of principles derived from psychoanalytic theory that disorder is the product of parent-child interactions in early life), most behavior therapists see the importance of the therapeutic relationship in narrower terms. They recognize the value of such features as promotion of trust because of the therapist's training and the caring shown by the therapist, the reinforcement value of being understood and accepted when in distress, the value of the collaborative nature of the relationship, and positive attributes of the teaching role (for example, in anxiety-reduction techniques and assertive training).

Despite stereotypes to the contrary, behavioral therapies are based on beliefs consistent with the human potential movement. It is believed that, under the right circumstances, people are capable of making positive changes. Freud's theories fit more squarely with the Judeo-Christian beliefs in the fall of humankind, positing basic internal conflicts as the root of emotional disturbance. This distinction between behaviorism and psychoanalysis is manifest in the behavioral rejection of the medical model as well as in the differing procedures used in the therapy office. Behavioral therapists work collaboratively with clients, believing that the client has equal input into the process of therapy. Behaviorists have no secrets from their clients; they are not interested in insight or interpretations of client's verbalizations, but rather in developing a list of targets for behavior change and engaging the client in developing a plan of change.

The case illustrations in Chapter 5 should give a sense of the wide array of problems treated by behavior therapists, the interactive quality of the therapy situation, and the kind of behavioral analyses that take place. What is unique about behavior therapy is its insistence on experimentally established procedures. Here are a few examples of some behavioral techniques that frequently are used in the course of therapy:

1. Relaxation training. There is a long history of the use of deep muscle relaxation as a means of reducing anxiety. Jacobson (1929), a physician, did pioneering work on this technique based on his recognition that increasing muscle relaxation induced a state that is incompatible with the muscular tension that accompanies the experience of anxiety.

There have been numerous experimental demonstrations of its value (Goldfried & Trier, 1974; Paul, 1969). Wolpe's systematic desensitization technique for unlearning phobias made use of deep muscle relaxation to counteract anxiety. The case of the person with the elevator phobia in Chapter 5 is representative of cases where relaxation training is likely to be one of the techniques employed.

2. Behavioral rehearsal. This type of procedure is aimed at providing the client with direct training in the specific social performance skills that are missing. Assertiveness training is an example, where a therapist, in collaboration with the client, puts together certain exercises that enable the client to learn to take appropriate actions toward a desired goal. Target situations are identified, practice takes place (sometimes using role-play to improve the desired behavior), followed by carrying out the new behaviors outside the therapy situation in the client's real life. Assessments are conducted of the experience to fine-tune and establish the new behavior so that it is maintained after therapy ends. The case of the lonely man in Chapter 5 is representative of cases where behavioral rehearsal might be one of the techniques used.

3. Relabeling. How a person responds to a situation emotionally is often the result of how the situation is cognitively labeled by that person. Behavior therapists help their clients to become aware of assumptions about situations, and they encourage and help clients select behaviors to test these assumptions rather than simply taking them for granted. Effort is directed toward identifying areas where supposedly factually based views of the client come to be understood through new experiences as assumptions, enabling the initiation of new behavior that is more adaptive. The case of the fear of failure in Chapter 5 is representative of cases where relabeling might be one of the techniques employed.

4. Exposure. A number of disorders are best addressed by arranging for prolonged contact with the object of irrational fears, breaking up the avoidance pattern. People suffering from obsessive-compulsive disorders are most effectively treated by having them handle objects they believe to be contaminated (Foa & Kozack, 1986). Similarly, people with a fear of heights often overcome their fear when they engage in a series of graded experiences at increasing heights. The case of hand-washing in Chapter 5 is representative of cases where an exposure technique is likely to be used.

In many ways, behavior therapy is an educational process. It is a teaching situation involving two people who actively participate to identify problems, select means to address these problems using empirically derived procedures, and promote the initiation of new, more adaptive behaviors to replace what have been maladaptive behaviors.

Behavioral Activation

Taking the work of Ferster a step beyond a behavioral explanation for depression, Peter Lewinsohn developed a system for applying the behavioral principles to clinical settings in the treatment of depression. His method for treating depression was called behavioral activation. Because depression often results from low levels of positive reinforcement and high levels of punishment, Lewinsohn and colleagues (Lewinsohn, 1974) sought to increase positive reinforcement in peoples' lives through behavioral activation. They developed an instrument called the Pleasant Events Schedule (MacPhillamy & Lewinsohn, 1972, 1982) that consisted of a long list of reinforcing events—also referred to as "pleasant events"—to measure the presence or absence of such events in peoples' lives. The goal of behavioral activation for depression at this time was to help clients schedule pleasant events into their weeks. The more pleasant events the depressed client scheduled and engaged in, the more reinforcing life would become. As the negative experiences decreased and reinforcing experiences increased, there was a decrease in depression. Like other behavioral models, Lewinsohn's approach proposed that clients engage in activities that were counter to depressive and punishing activities. It is rare for a person to be engaged in a pleasant activity and feel depressed, just as it is difficult to be relaxed and anxious at the same time, which you will recall was the theory behind systematic desensitization, one of the earliest behavior therapies.

Chapter 5 provides case illustrations of how behavioral activation is applied to instigate specific actions that have been missing because of negatively reinforced avoidance behavior. Lewinsohn's work has been updated in the sense that the most important positive activities to be promoted are regarded as those that have been lost to the particular individual as a result of learned avoidance. As well as promoting pleasant activities, behavior therapists working in this way to treat depression seek to promote the growth of such corrective activities as the primary means of improving the lives of their clients.

Cognitive-Behavior Therapy

At the same time that Ferster, Lewinsohn, and others (for example, Bellack, Hersen, & Himmelhoch, 1981; Rehm, 1977) were developing successful behavioral treatments for depression, other psychologists and psychiatrists were looking at how the way people think influences their moods. Psychiatrist Aaron T. Beck, originally trained in psychoanalytic theory, noticed that his depressed patients demonstrated stereotypically negative thoughts about the world, themselves, and their futures. He developed cognitive therapy for depression (Beck, 1976; Beck, Rush, Shaw, & Emery, 1979) as a method for modifying these negative automatic thoughts. Simultaneously and independently, psychologist Albert Ellis developed a cognitive approach to treatment called rational emotive therapy (Ellis, 1962) as a general approach to treatment, not specific to the treatment of depression. Early in treatment, therapists utilize the behavioral activation techniques developed by Lewinsohn, such as activity scheduling, to assist depressed clients who are particularly lethargic and withdrawn.

The most important components of cognitive therapy are the modification of dysfunctional thoughts. Beck and his colleagues identified three types of thoughts: automatic thoughts that are situation specific—a letter from your mother arrives in the mail and you think "oh, no, bad news is on the way;" underlying assumptions and conditional beliefs that arise in multiple situations such as "I should always be a kind person" or "if I am nice to everyone, people will like me;" and core beliefs that are proposed to be enduring, cross-situational, and absolutist beliefs about the self and the world such as "I am incompetent." Cognitive-behavioral approaches to therapy aim to identify and correct these assumptions and beliefs that trigger negative emotions and interfere with constructive behavior.

Many studies support the use of cognitive-behavior therapy with depressed clients. The treatment usually outperforms pill placebo or waiting-list control groups. Cognitive-behavioral therapy is considered an empirically supported treatment by the American Psychological Association's Division of Clinical Psychology (Division 12) that requires such treatments to be supported by research at multiple locations and replicated in multiple studies (Chambless et al., 1998). Therapists with more experience and training have been shown to have superior success (DeRubeis et al., 2005). Although antidepressant medication may work faster and initially demonstrate slightly superior outcomes to cognitive-behavior therapy (DeRubeis et al., 2005), both treatments are useful with moderately to severely depressed clients, contrary to popular medical treatment guidelines suggesting that medication should be the first choice with moderately to severely depressed clients. Furthermore, in a 12-month follow-up to a comparison study between cognitive therapy and paroxetine (Paxil), only 30.8 percent of the cognitive therapy patients relapsed after treatment was ended, whereas 76.2 percent of clients originally treated with paroxetine relapsed once the medication was discontinued (Hollon et al., 2005). This suggests that cognitive therapy has a more enduring effect than antidepressant medication.

Behavior Therapy versus Other Forms of Psychotherapy

There is the question of whether behavior therapy is more helpful than other approaches to psychotherapy. It is not unusual to read that there is no difference in the effectiveness of different forms of psychotherapy, and some research reports have backed that up. According to this assessment, all psychotherapies are deemed effective, but no particular form of therapy is comparatively more effective. One well-known and often-cited study compared psychodynamic psychotherapy with behavior therapy and concluded that there was no difference between them (Sloane, Staples, Cristol, Yorkston, & Whipple, 1975). However, a subsequent meta-analysis that looked more carefully at these results found that behavioral treatment outperformed nonbehavioral treatments (Giles, 1983a, 1983b). In fact, in eight of the nine areas that were being studied, the results with behavior therapy were significantly better. Similar results favoring behavior therapy were obtained by Giles when he statistically examined three other comparative studies that initially found no differences between treatment modalities (Giles, 1983b, pp. 30–31). Another analysis comparing behavior therapy with psychodynamic therapy yielded the same results favoring the effectiveness of behavior therapy (Andrews & Harvey, 1981). Thus, there is reason to believe that all therapies are not equal. While the results for psychotherapy are good, the results for behavior therapy have been shown to be better.

Behavior Therapy versus Pharmacotherapy

While behavioral approaches to therapy continued to be popular among academic, research-oriented psychologists, many practicing clinicians were strongly influenced by cognitive therapy during the 1980s. Because cognitive therapies also make use of such behavioral techniques as activity scheduling, relaxation training, and social skills training in conjunction with the modification of beliefs, the technique came to be known as cognitive-behavior therapy (CBT). CBT is now one of the most widely studied treatment approaches for a variety of problems ranging from depression to obsessive-compulsive disorder. Furthermore, it is one of the few therapies that has consistently performed as well as, or outperformed, medication in the treatment of depression in a number of controlled clinical trials.

In summarizing the efficacy research on CBT for depression, Craighead, Craighead, and Ilardi (1998, p. 229) state that:

> With the possible exception of [one major study—discussed below], the essential finding in all these studies is that CBT is equally effective to antidepressant medication in alleviating [major depressive disorder] among outpatients.... Typically, 50–70% of (these) patients who complete a course of CBT no longer meet the criteria for (major depressive disorder) at posttreatment.

The study that questioned the efficacy of cognitive-behavioral therapy in the treatment of depression to which Craighead and colleagues refer (Elkin et al., 1989) has had major consequences for the treatment of depression because it led to the establishment of guidelines by the American Psychiatric Association that are now standard for the psychiatric and medical communities. The study found that, whereas the drug (imipramine hydrochloride) was superior in its effectiveness to placebo, cognitive-behavior therapy was not. However, subsequent analyses of this study have questioned this interpretation and challenged the guidelines as unwarranted. The study's results were highly variable and distinctively different, depending upon the site of the study, such that averaging of totals across sites masked these differences (Jacobson & Hollon, 1996).

Other data show no statistical difference in the effectiveness of behavior therapy versus medication (Persons, Thase, & Crits-Christoph, 1996). The treatments for depression study conducted by Jacobson and colleagues demonstrated once again that there was no advantage of medication over either cognitive behavioral therapy or behavioral activation for severely depressed patients (Dimidjian et al., 2003). In addition, the cognitive-behavioral and behavioral activation conditions had fewer dropouts from therapy than did the medication condition, suggesting the presence of unpleasant features to being on medication. More patients receiving behavioral activation treatment reached full remission of depressive symptoms than in other conditions. Although more research is needed to determine which patients are likely to do better with cognitive therapy or with behavioral activation or, for that matter, medication, the guidelines that suggest that medication should be the first treatment with more severely depressed patients are contradicted by these studies and subsequent reanalyses of the study often cited to justify the preference for drug treatment. It should be clear from a review of the literature that the American Psychiatric Association has underemphasized multiple studies of the effectiveness of behavioral treatments for depression.

The site differences in the outcome of CBT for the treatment of depression suggest that CBT is a complex therapy requiring thorough training to be delivered effectively. More research is needed into the best means of ensuring the quality of care offered by this treatment. Some recent data, however, raise the question of how important the cognitive elements are for the treatment's success. A study has indicated that the value of CBT is attributable to the behavioral component, questioning the importance of the contribution of cognitive elements of the treatment in effecting change (Jacobson et al., 1996). It may be that cognitive elements are important for describing the nature of the problem with a patient, but have less value in their own right as a means of eliminating the problem. In what way the effective components of treatment are cognitive as well as behavioral is a question still to be answered by future research. A treatment manual has now been written for behavioral activation that updates Lewinsohn's (1974) approach with an emphasis on modifying avoidance behavior (Martell, Addis, & Jacobson, 2001) that should be an important aid in training therapists to provide cognitive therapy and that will be helpful in settling this question.

What About the Placebo Effect?

Chapter 2 reviewed the research on pharmacological treatment and presented reasons to conclude that the success of this therapy is explainable in large part, if not entirely, as the result of a placebo effect. Although a number of studies have suggested a superiority of behavioral treatment over drug treatment, other studies show no difference between the results of these two approaches. If the drug results are largely or even fully attributable to a placebo effect, why does this not apply equally to behavioral treatments? There is every reason to believe that some of the effect of behavioral treatment is a placebo effect. It is natural for all of us to want to believe in our helpers and to attribute value to their advice. Hope is an important ingredient in promoting change. The answer to this question hinges on whether there is a substantial contribution beyond the placebo effect. Several points are pertinent in considering this issue. We know that behavioral treatment has consistently shown superiority in its endurance following treatment when compared to drug treatments. Relapse is common after withdrawal of drugs, whereas behavioral treatment, because it teaches new coping behaviors, retains its value far better after treatment has ended. We also can point to a sound theoretical and empirical basis for the behavioral treatments, with substantiated mechanisms governing the approach, that is absent when it comes to pharmacological therapy. Unlike drug treatment, behavioral methods have been developed out of lines of empirical research that led to the specific techniques developed and give credence to these techniques. Finally, while there is reason in double-blind studies to point to the physical effects of the drug inducing a placebo effect rather than a real effect, there is no question about the reality of the adverse physical side effects of these drugs. The behavioral treatments pose no such immediate, and perhaps later erupting, dangers.

Words and Emotions

Behaviorists look to experiments with animals to understand how human cognition differs from lower mammals. A theory called "relational frame theory" extends the early Skinnerian theories of verbal behavior (Skinner, 1957) to explain how human language influences human emotion (Hayes, Barnes-Holmes, & Roche, 2001). According to relational frame theory, thoughts do not cause behavior, because thoughts *are* behavior. Events take on stimulus properties of other events, so words that we use to describe a traumatizing event such as the death of a loved one contain similar properties as the original event itself, and the words elicit similar emotions. In this way, humans cause themselves to reexperience pain over and over again. Yet humans also work hard to avoid emotional pain. Thus, the negative properties acquired by words elicit negative emotional responses, and avoidance of negative emotional responses leads to the types of behaviors of withdrawal and inertia that describe depression. Although the behavioral explanation of cognition is not at this time widely recognized in the field of psychology, attempts to provide a clearer understanding of emotional disorders are underway. To date CBT, broadly practiced, is one of the most effective treatments for depression and anxiety disorders. Nevertheless, increasing medicalization in the behavioral health field has led to guidelines that favor medication interventions over well-researched and successful psychosocial treatments.

Co-morbidity

As discussed earlier, the diagnostic system for mental disorders has become increasingly specific and may refer to categories of broader underlying syndromes rather than discrete or unique disorders (Barlow, Allen, & Choate, 2004). Research suggests that there is considerable overlap in conditions. In one study, as many as 76 percent of patients that met criteria for an anxiety or mood disorder met criteria for a co-occurring diagnosis of either another anxiety or depressive disorder or some other condition (Brown, Campbell, Lehman, Grisham, & Mancill, 2001). When there is such a high degree of co-morbidity, one has further reason to wonder whether the distinctions made in psychiatric diagnosis are as useful as they are purported to be.

When one further considers that drug treatments such as SSRIs—though not the panacea that they are touted to be—are used to treat depression, anxiety, obsessions, and other problems and that cognitive behavioral therapy also is being applied to the treatment of multiple problems, the question of whether the same processes are at work in many of these disorders needs to be considered. Barlow, Allen, and Choate (2004) did just that. These researchers suggest that common to many disorders such as anxiety and depression are antecedent appraisal of internal or external threats and danger that effect the expression of negative emotion, emotional avoidance, and modifying emotional action tendencies. In other words, in many of the emotional disorders, people react to their appraisal of threat or danger and act to avoid negative feelings. Behavioral and cognitive-behavioral treatments modify these action tendencies (such as avoiding a feared object like a snake or becoming passive and apathetic when depressed). It is possible that SSRIs blunt negative emotion in general and are therefore useful in helping people suffering from a variety of "diagnoses" to feel better. It would be very desirable for future diagnostic systems to take these common factors into account. The specificity of our current diagnostic system creates the illusion of many discrete "mental illnesses." Thus, it sounds rational to say that "depression is an illness" or that "you have a social phobia." All of these disorders may be better represented under the heading of a "negative affect syndrome" (Barlow, Allen, & Choate, 2004); considering any of the manifestations to be a discrete illness is less plausible.

What is central in all of these conditions characterized by negative affect—that is objectively verifiable—is the presence of avoidance behavior.

Explaining Depression

So now we return again to the crux of this book. Why do people become depressed? Are you depressed because you have a chemical imbalance? Although neurotransmitter levels appear to be associated with depression, there is little evidence to suggest that they cause depression or anxiety or other disorders. Is negative thinking the culprit? Insofar as our thinking, the words we speak to ourselves, are associated with negative experiences and take on the aversive properties of those experiences, thoughts certainly contribute to negative mood. Is depression your problem at all? Are you one of the thousands of people who experience both depression and anxiety and possibly become obsessive about keeping your house neat or ruminate over your heartaches and losses? Our answer is this: a plethora of data exist to suggest that depression is the result of life events, negative responses to life events, avoidance of negative emotion, and the limitations on life that avoidance creates.

If depression is part of a negative affect syndrome characterized by evaluating situations as threatening or dangerous and acting to avoid such aversive consequences, what sense does it make to turn to medication as the answer? Millions of people turn to medications to make themselves feel better. It is ironic that when a physician prescribes a drug that elevates mood we call it a "treatment of choice," but when a drug dealer on the street sells a block of crack cocaine to elevate mood we put him or her in prison. Certainly, the requirement for prescriptions of controlled substances to remedy illnesses is to protect the public, and there is no argument here in that regard. However, when people who get drunk or high on drugs are told by professionals that they are "self-medicating" and their physician then prescribes a medication because it has a euphoric impact, we are operating with an odd inconsistency as a society. Wouldn't it be better to learn to cope with life more effectively rather than attempt to blot it or ourselves out?

What about the viewpoint that bad moods, fears, sadness, and unpleasantness are just a part of life? Such a concept goes back to ancient Stoic and Epicurean philosophies, although those ancient thinkers placed a morbid emphasis on enduring pain and suffering as a means of spiritual fulfillment. Simply accepting pain and suffering, however, is clearly out of vogue in the hedonistic twenty-first century, when the dictum is still primarily, "if it feels good, do it." Behavior therapy can help individuals take action to improve their lives despite their negative feelings. CBT can help people to become less reactive to their appraisals of situations as bad or dangerous. Embracing, rather than avoiding, a broad range of emotion and considering what you value in life and moving toward those valued things is a reasonable approach. Representing this philosophy, one newer behavior therapy approach called acceptance and commitment therapy (Hayes, Strosahl, & Wilson, 1999) teaches people to give up their struggle against negative emotion, to accept life as it is, and to commit themselves to actions leading to a life that they highly value.

Behaviorism, the hard-headed, experimental field of psychology that has been so maligned as overly clinical and cold, presents methods for living that have similarities to what religions and philosophers have promoted for centuries. While we saw in Chapter 1 how many of these superstitious ideas were harmful, perhaps there was some wisdom as well. The cognitive therapy emphasis on countering negative beliefs with a more positive outlook is not all that far from the biblical suggestion in the letter to the Philippians of dwelling on "whatever is true, whatever is honorable, whatever is just, whatever is pure, whatever is pleasing, whatever is commendable, if there is any excellence and if there is anything worthy of praise" (NRSV, 1990).

Behavioral activation and acceptance and commitment therapy, while not promoting suffering as an ascetic ideal, and while certainly not advocating capitulation to misery, do have elements that hearken back to Stoic philosophy. Many things in life must be endured and overcome, and one can live a good life despite some suffering. While the suggestion that there is similarity between religion or philosophy and behavior therapy may cause some readers to recall images of people having demons cast from them for being socially odd, it should not be surprising that social science may have brought us back to some wisdom from the ages. However, we now are in a position to apply the scientific method to keep us from straying from data that tell us whether our methodologies are useful.

The medical model carries the mantel of science, but it has no more claim to the scientific method than the learning model of social science. In fact, as we have pointed out, many of the conclusions drawn from the pharmacotherapy literature are circular, and the marketing that promotes drugs as the only proven treatments is easily revealed to be importantly motivated by profit rather than care.

Your Choice

People have a choice in the matter of how to help themselves. Too little is said in the popular press about nonpharmaceutical choices for dealing with depression and anxiety. Certainly, CBT and other approaches have not been shown to be a fast fix, but they have demonstrated efficacy and endurance over time. Medication, on the other hand, while bringing about rapid improvement in some cases, does not produce enduring effects when the medication is discontinued and can be associated with negative side effects. Learning stays with us, and behavior therapies, based on learning principles, are designed to endure over time and in multiple situations. We believe that to be the outcome of choice.

CHAPTER 7

SUMMARY AND CONCLUSIONS

The last 20 years have seen an enormous increase in the diagnosis and pharmacological treatment of depression. A recent survey showed that one out of three office visits by women includes prescription of an antidepressant drug. How should we explain this phenomenon? One possible explanation is that we are in the midst of an unprecedented epidemic of depression. Another is that we have suddenly become very good at detecting depression. Neither explanation has merit, and there is reason to be concerned that we don't know what we are doing.

The answers to what is driving this are to be found in (1) adoption by the field of psychiatry of a belief in a biochemical basis for depression that has enabled psychiatry to recover from a state of alarming decline by the 1980s into becoming a robust medical specialty; (2) the highly sophisticated marketing by the pharmaceutical industry to doctors and the general public of psychotropic drugs that has led to enormous profits for the industry; (3) acceptance within the professional community by medical doctors (internists, family physicians, gynecologists) and most mental health practitioners (psychologists and social workers, as well as psychiatrists) of a biological explanation for depression as a disease that is the result of a defect in brain chemistry and as a disorder that can be fixed by a drug; and (4) a similar acceptance by the general public and the media of this explanation.

The biological explanation for depression (and other mental disorders not discussed in this book) is an extension of thinking derived from

136The Myth of Depression as Disease

the great advances that have been made in the last 150 years in the diagnosis and treatment of physical disorders. The approach that was taken in making these impressive advances, which led to validation of the medical model, owed its success to the gradual accumulation of knowledge about anatomy, physiology, and biochemistry. This strategy, regularly verified through controlled experiments, enabled researchers to come to an understanding of how symptoms of illness could be related to underlying physiological causes, thereby enabling the development of treatments that addressed these causes.

The mental health field has adopted this same model in its attempts to explain mental disorder. Sometimes it has done so by devising psychological theories of causation, at other times by proposing organic theories. For half a century, psychoanalysis, a psychological theory based on the medical model, dominated the field by postulating underlying causes for mental disorders traceable to childhood experiences that produced unconscious conflicts and symptoms. There have been many variations of psychoanalytic thinking. Modern psychodynamic theory poses many credible theories of the impact of infant attachment on emotional development and the experience of the self. Much has been made of psychosocial development and the interaction of interpersonal processes and development. Research on the impact of these theories on treatment success has not been conducted. One extension of these theories has been researched and applied in the treatment of depression, and interpersonal psychotherapy (IPT) is a promising treatment based on many of the principles that are posited in psychodynamic or interpersonal theories (Klerman, Weissman, Rounsaville, & Chevron, 1984). Ironically, IPT is an effective psychosocial treatment for depression that utilizes the medical model as explanation. Even within the acceptance of the medical model, nonpharmacological approaches have demonstrated success.

For the past quarter century, a biological theory has held sway as the accepted medical model. According to this theory, deficiencies in various neurotransmitters in the brain are the cause of different mental disorders. In the case of depression, the neurotransmitter serotonin is cited. However, in contrast to the history of the development of an understanding of physical illnesses, where the medical model was the outcome of systematic research that established objective connections between symptoms and their underlying causes, the adoption of this model to explain mental disorder has been based on speculations and theories rather than facts. There have been no discoveries to substantiate an underlying state that support either this model or the use of the drug treatments currently in vogue.

It is a simple fact that the biological explanation on which all of this is based is missing a sound scientific basis. There is much window dressing, but not much substance to the claims that have been made and widely accepted. Scrutiny of the research on antidepressant drugs reveals that the great bulk of the effect (at least 80 percent) is likely due to a placebo effect, with reason to suspect that the unaccounted for portion may be a specious contribution attributable to the intrusive practices of the drug companies that support almost all of the reported results. In addition, undesirable and potentially dangerous side effects of these drugs have been consistently under-reported by the drug companies. Concerns are heightened by the discovery, highlighted through congressional hearings, that the Food and Drug Administration has failed in its mission to monitor these drugs once they have been approved. There is reason for concern that there may be serious long-term negative consequences that will be experienced by the great numbers of people now taking antidepressant drugs. Further complicating the picture is the existence of an antiquated system of diagnoses that is woefully unreliable as a means of classifying problems of mental disorder when compared with the system used for diagnosis in physical medicine.

Fortunately, a ray of hope in this picture is the existence of an alternative treatment—behavior therapy that has been demonstrated to have as much or more success than drugs. Studies have shown that behavior therapy provides remedies that are longer-lasting and pose no concerns regarding side effects. Unlike the drug treatments, behavior therapy has evolved out of a solid base in research. The behavioral therapies are based on a different conceptual model, a learning model that looks at the context in which the disorder occurs and that appears to have greater merit in explaining the basis for depression (and other mental disorders). Furthermore, this model indicates specifically how depression should be treated by accounting for the disorder as the outcome of avoidance behavior, a well-understood process by virtue of a great deal of behavioral research. One behavioral treatment, behavioral activation, has been shown to yield particularly good results. Another behavioral treatment, cognitive-behavioral therapy, was also found to yield very good results. CBT attends to thinking as part of the treatment and has been widely studied, validated, and disseminated.

Unlike the negative emotional states of fear and grief, which are easily understood as having survival value, it is difficult to make a case for depression as an evolutionary selected state. In this sense, fear and grief appear to be primary emotional states, whereas depression seems better conceptualized as a secondary state—a reaction to a reaction. Behavioral treatments have successfully addressed depression from this standpoint rather than viewing depression as a disease.

The time has come to recognize the mythology that surrounds current views of the effectiveness of psychiatric drugs with respect to the treatment of depression and other disorders. People seeking help need better information about the choices available to them and the pros and cons associated with those choices. Doctors making referrals for treatment need to be better informed about these same issues so they make better referrals. There is a similar need to educate mental health practitioners who deliver treatment and the managed care industry which determines what treatments are covered. It is important that the media do a better job of reporting the true state of affairs with respect to theories and treatments pertaining to depression. Finally, federal support for research must also be more cognizant of the scientific issues involved so that research into behavioral treatment, which has received a tiny fraction of the support accorded to drug treatment, is better funded in order to accelerate continued development of treatment methods.

Taking medication improves many problems (for example stomach ulcers) that behavioral change (that is, a bland diet) could also improve over time. Surely, humane treatment providers would not deny faster methods to alleviate suffering. The same is true for antidepressant medications. The problem, however, is that few people are able to take them without annoying side effects such as sexual dysfunction or dry mouth that need to be either managed by more medication or simply tolerated. Another problem is that the medications do not work for everyone. And there is the problem that quite often discontinuation of drugs leads to relapse because no new behavior has been learned to ward off depression. If you are one of the millions of people that have tried one antidepressant to no avail, and then another and another, ultimately coming to believe that your situation is so hopeless that even drugs don't work, you understand the frustration of hearing the promise of cure and finding none. Life is lived one day at a time, with small changes in behavior often resulting in big improvements in the experience of life. Changes can happen sometimes from the inside (through a medication) or the outside (behavior change), or through some combination. Television advertisements suggesting that all your social anxieties, depressed moods, and dysphoria can be erased by a pill suggest a panacea for human ills. There is no such panacea, in medicine or in psychology. There is hope, however. Research has consistently demonstrated that cognitive and behavioral treatments lead to successful outcomes, whether the problem is depression or anxiety. Does it work for everybody? No, nothing does. However, as an informed public, it is important to know the alternatives and that nonbiological treatments have been shown to be at least as good, or superior, to medications. It may take a little longer, but the outcomes are also more likely to endure.

The old expression that all good things take time has lost favor as we expect instantaneous results. People can enter the hospital for major surgery and leave in relatively good condition within a few days, when they once would have been bedridden for weeks. We expect change now, this instant, like dinner from a microwave. However, as our world has increased in pace, so has the complaint of meaninglessness, isolation, and depression in society. Rather than attempting to medicate away these problems, it may be a better choice to take the time to improve life, engage in it fully, and find meaning in the experiences of joy and pain to which all human beings are subject.

Questions to Ask before Accepting a Prescription for Antidepressant Medication

The days of "the doctor knows best" are long gone and patients need to educate themselves and advocate for themselves when seeing a physician. Complicated technology, the plethora of new medications coming to the market monthly, and increased demands on physicians' time make it nearly impossible for them to keep up with current literature, and they frequently rely on representatives (that is, salespeople) from pharmaceutical companies to tell them about the literature on medications that they will eventually prescribe to their patients. Pharmaceutical representatives (salespeople) are required to attend seminars about the drugs they sell, their effectiveness, and side effects. Make no mistake about it, however, these seminars are conducted by the pharmaceutical company and are equal parts marketing and scientific information. These salespeople are not doctors or nurses, nor are they scientists. They are typically young, attractive salespeople who make a commission on the amount of product that they sell. It is up to the patient, therefore, to ask the right questions of his or her physician to ensure that both doctor and patient are well informed about the medications being suggested. Below are several questions that can help in a patient's decision to accept or reject a prescription for antidepressant medications.

1. Not infrequently, primary care doctors will diagnose a patient with depression based on very little information. Patients reporting difficulty sleeping, fatigue, sadness, or difficulty concentrating, or any combination of those problems are often prescribed antidepressant

medication without further investigation into possible causes for such problems. If your doctor suggests that you try an antidepressant medication, the first question to ask is, "On what basis do you find that I am depressed?" A physician would not send you for a liver biopsy without fairly conclusive evidence by less intrusive means that there is a problem with your liver. There are no blood tests for depression, however, and diagnoses are made and pills prescribed on fairly scant evidence. Make sure your doctor can provide a good rationale for giving you a diagnosis of a mental health problem before accepting the presumed quick fix.

2. Should you believe that you are, indeed, depressed, your doctor should be able to tell you why he or she is prescribing a particular medication. The doctor should also be able to tell you why he or she is prescribing any medication at all. Ask your doctor what the literature says about the effectiveness of the medication prescribed. "What percentage of research participants actually improved in studies conducted on the use of this medicine? How many stay improved after they have discontinued the medicine?" Research studies give general averages of outcome with drugs or therapy. Also ask your doctor how many of his or her patients improve with any particular medication alone, and how often your doctor needs to change medications and dosages before finding one that helps. If the doctor cannot answer to your satisfaction, you might consider alternatives to the medication.

3. Pharmaceutical companies report common side effects on labeling of their products. However, there are often individual case reports that do not appear on labels. Ask your doctor if any of his or her patients have reported side effects that may not be commonly reported. What, if any, rare but troubling side effects have they heard about at professional conferences and seminars? Your doctor is likely to want to reassure you that the drugs he or she is prescribing are not dangerous. Make it clear that you are not asking out of fear that the doctor is giving you something harmful, but rather that you want to make an informed decision about what you put in your body and the side effects you are willing to experience for the sake of trying a pill that may improve your mood.

4. If your doctor gave you a prescription for a diet pill or sent you to a surgeon for liposuction because she believed you needed to lose 20 pounds, you might first ask, "Are there other means of weight loss that I might try first, such as changing my diet and exercise?" By far the most important question anyone can ask a doctor before taking a psychopharmacological medication is, "Are there alternative treatments that I should try first?" Your doctor should know the literature that compares drug treatments for depression to cognitive-behavioral therapy and interpersonal therapy. If he or she does not, perhaps he or

she should not prescribe medication for psychological problems, and it might be time to make a proper referral to a behavioral health specialist. Medications are not cheaper than therapy in the long run (Antonuccio, Thomas, & Danton, 1997), although many people are reluctant to pay to talk to a therapist. Remember that most insurance companies pay a portion of the bill for psychotherapy.

Appendix B

How to Find a Behavioral or Cognitive-behavioral Therapist

Due to the demonstrated success of cognitive and behavioral therapies, more and more therapists are implementing these techniques with their clients. Insurance companies expect that treatment will be relatively short-term and have proven efficacy. For this reason, many people write cognitive-behavioral treatments into their treatment plans but do not necessarily utilize the theories behind the techniques, or they lack sufficient training to implement the techniques successfully. Some therapists believe that if they use any one procedure, such as having a client evaluate the validity of his or her thoughts, they are doing cognitive-behavioral therapy (CBT). For this reason, it is important to find someone who holds a cognitive-behavioral theoretical orientation in conceptualizing treatment plans and who has had sufficient training in the techniques to skillfully conduct therapy. Although certainty about a therapist's skill cannot be gained apart from working with the therapist, here are several recommendations for finding proper referrals to behavioral or cognitive-behavioral therapists:

Professional Organizations

At the national level, several professional organizations either consist of CBT researchers and practitioners or have sections that focus on CBT. The primary, multidisciplinary organization for behavioral and cognitive-behavioral practitioners is the Association of Behavioral and Cognitive Therapies (ABCT), formerly known as the Association for Advancement of Behavior Therapy. Membership in ABCT is open to all behavioral health specialties and includes psychologists, social workers, psychiatrists, nurses, and mental health counselors, as well as students in those fields. The association maintains a Web site (www.aabt.org) that includes search capabilities for finding behavioral and cognitive-behavioral therapists internationally.

With membership restricted to psychologists, the American Board of Professional Psychology (ABPP) is the primary national certification board for advanced competence in a variety of specialty areas. The ABPP has specialty board certification in cognitive-behavioral psychology. Board-certified CBT therapists can be located through the ABPP Web site at www.abpp.org.

Another certifying body specific to cognitive therapy is the multi-disciplinary Academy of Cognitive Therapy. Certified cognitive therapists can be found at www.academyofct.org.

Finally, the International Association of Cognitive Psychotherapy can be located at www.cognitivetherapyassociation.org.

Finding a Behavioral Therapist Locally

There are several methods for finding behavioral or cognitive-behavioral therapists at the local level without resorting to a yellow page advertisement. Many state and provincial psychological associations or other professional associations maintain referral services, and providers are asked to state their theoretical orientation. Likewise, many insurance companies and insurance provider panels ask the same of their practitioners. Because a provider may list CBT as one of many orientations, this is a less assured way of finding someone who understands the theory and keeps abreast of the research. A provider may primarily work from a psychodynamic or humanistic framework and use minimal CBT techniques, but will still appear in a referral list as a CBT therapist. It is a good idea to interview therapists briefly before making an appointment; Appendix C provides some questions to ask a therapist before beginning therapy.

Many, although not all, university departments of psychology have professors who are behaviorists and cognitive-behaviorists. Certain universities have clinical centers that are identified as CBT training clinics—for example, the Center for Cognitive Therapy at the University of Pennsylvania is well known for being a center of excellence in cognitive therapy. Calling a department of psychology or counseling and asking whether they train students in CBT is a good way to find graduates from such programs who may practice locally.

There are also private-practice settings that have been formed by therapists who share a particular therapeutic orientation. Look for practices with names like "Center for Cognitive Therapy" or "Institute of Behavior Therapy," as such places usually hire and/or train people in cognitive or behavioral techniques. Other words that indicate that people have training in behavioral or cognitive behavioral therapies are "Rational Emotive Behavior Therapy" or "Applied Behavior Analysis." The term "behavioral health" is used broadly as an alternative to "mental health," which is sometimes regarded as pejorative or as implying a dualistic mind-body approach. The presence of the term "behavioral" may not indicate that a practitioner is a behavioral or cognitive-behavioral therapist.

Appendix C

Questions to Ask a Potential Behavioral Therapist

As stated earlier, some therapists utilize cognitive and behavioral techniques but do not strongly adhere to the theory. It is usually better to find a therapist who follows a particular therapeutic approach; a therapist who believes the theory and follows the research promises more likely competence in the practice of a particular therapeutic orientation. Below are several questions that you can ask in a brief telephone interview and the types of answers that you will want to hear in order to help you choose a therapist.

1. Do you consider yourself a cognitive or behavioral therapist? You will want to ask this basic question. Expect that true cognitive or behavioral practitioners will state that this is their primary orientation and will be unlikely to make vague statements such as, "well, I do use that approach." Some people will consider themselves more cognitive, some more behavioral, others do not distinguish between the two; do not be overly concerned with that because the research is solid for a broad spectrum of behavioral and cognitive behavioral approaches.

2. Do you hold any certifications in the approach? Certification in a particular therapeutic approach is voluntary, and often expensive, so you should not rule out a therapist that does not answer affirmatively to this question. Some therapists have been awarded a diploma by the American Board of Professional Psychology (ABPP) on the basis of clinical experience beyond what is required for state licensure and completion of a rigorous examination. The ABPP designates board certification as a specialist in clinical and other areas of psychology, as well as the specialty in cognitive-behavioral psychology. However,

while the ABPP designation implies a high standard of performance as a therapist, such certification in clinical or counseling psychology, for example, does not require a behavioral orientation, and it is important to determine whether that is the case. Some of these therapists do have a behavioral orientation but have not pursued additional certification as a behavior therapist; others may offer some behavioral techniques but are more identified with some other orientation. If you are interviewing a therapist with an ABPP certification but no additional certification as a behavioral therapist, the answers given to the first question above will be particularly important, despite the specialty certification. However, when a therapist has received such certification, you can feel confident that your therapist has demonstrated proficiency in a technique if they have been examined through a certification process. Some certifying bodies or training institutes that evaluate proficiency of their trainees include:

> The Academy of Cognitive Therapy
> The American Board of Professional Psychology—Specialty Board in Cognitive-behavioral Therapy
> The Beck Institute for Cognitive Therapy and Research
> The Center for Cognitive Therapy—University of Pennsylvania (there are Centers for Cognitive Therapy in many cities and most provide excellent training; a therapist who has completed some form of postgraduate, comprehensive training at such a center is likely to be quite skilled in the approach)
> The Ellis Institute for Rational Emotive Behavior Therapy

3. Are your sessions relatively structured, and will you work with me to develop various assignments between sessions that will help me learn new behaviors or change the way I think during my regular week's activities? The answer should be an unequivocal "yes."
4. Do you follow a particular treatment protocol? Some cognitive-behavioral therapists follow protocols that have been validated through research for various problems. Others do not adhere to a "cookbook" but will tell you that they develop and follow a comprehensive CBT case formulation. Either answer can give you reasonable confidence that the therapist follows a CBT plan that he or she has developed through study of the research and through continuing education.

Always check the credentials of any therapist, making sure he or she has attended an accredited university or professional school and holds proper credentials to practice in your state of residence. Many licensing boards also can give you information regarding any complaints outstanding against a therapist, and you may wish to verify that the therapist is licensed or certified in good standing with your state board.

APPENDIX D

SUGGESTIONS FOR FURTHER READING

Many enlightening books have been written about the mental heath field and trends in treatment. Below is a brief annotated bibliography of books that readers may find interesting.

Szasz, T. (1974). *The myth of mental illness: Foundations of a theory of personal conduct* (rev. ed.). New York: HarperCollins.

This classic and controversial book has led some to ask of Dr. Szasz, "What kind of psychiatrist is he?" The work is iconoclastic and offers harsh criticism of societal control over human lives under the auspices of mental health treatment. His criticism deserved attention in the decade in which it was written, and it is still relevant today.

Valenstein, E. S. (1998). *Blaming the brain: The truth about drugs and mental health.* New York: Free Press.

Valenstein, a behavioral neuroscientist, presents a historical and critical account of the development and use of psychotropic medications in the mental health field. Citing research from psychiatry, neurology, and pharmacology, this work exposes the fallacies of the medical model as applied to behavioral problems. The book is even-handed, but forthright and powerfully convincing.

Whitaker, R. (2002). *Mad in America.* Cambridge, MA: Perseus.

This book is an excellent historical accounting of the treatment of the mentally ill in the United States. Whitaker's writing is engaging and brings the history to life. Describing the times of exorcizing demons to the days of de-institutionalization, the book illustrates the stark reality of the myths and misguided treatments sometimes proposed by well-meaning caregivers and at other times prescribed by people motivated by prejudice or power. It is a startling look, for the lay public, at the context from which the modern mental health system has sprung.

Our point has been to inform readers of choices available to them. In that vein, we offer the following reading list in behavioral and cognitive theories and therapy. This list is not comprehensive by any means, but it contains readable, basic material to help evaluate treatment options. Readers will also find these books valuable in helping them to evaluate their physician's and therapist's advice and prescriptions regarding treatment of emotional and behavioral problems.

Alberti, R., & Emmons, M. (2001). *Your perfect right* (8th ed.). San Luis Obispo, CA: Impact.

Focused on teaching assertiveness skills, this classic work has been a mainstay in the behavioral self-help literature since the first edition. It is a useful reference for people seeking to understand how behavior therapy can help with social anxieties, shyness, or difficulties being appropriately assertive.

Barlow, D. H., & Craske, M. G. (2000). *Mastery of your anxiety and panic* (3rd ed.). Albany, NY: Graywind Publications.

This workbook presents an empirically supported behavioral treatment for anxiety disorders and panic disorders. It is one of a number of similar workbooks by the same publisher that deal with a variety of anxiety issues.

Beck, A. T. (1976). *Cognitive therapy and the emotional disorders.* New York: International Universities Press.

One of the first comprehensive presentations of cognitive theory of emotional problems, this book was the initial presentation of Beck's revolutionary model. It is easily accessible to readers and complete with case examples.

Ellis, A., & Harper, R. A. (1975). *A new guide to rational living.* Englewood Cliffs, NJ: Prentice-Hall.

This guide presents rational emotive behavior therapy to a wide audience. It has been used by therapists and general readers alike to learn how a cognitive/rational approach to life's problems can moderate emotional distress.

Skinner, B. F. (1974). *About behaviorism.* New York: Alfred Knopf.

For readers interested in understanding the principles of behavioral psychology, this book from the preeminent behaviorist of the twentieth century serves as a good beginning point. Skinner presents theory and application of behaviorism as well as the professional context in which the field of behavioral analysis developed.

The following workbooks provide self-help for people dealing with depression and other difficulties. They are based on principles of cognitive and behavioral theory. Most of the books are written as adjunctive guides rather than as replacements for consultation with trained behavioral health professionals.

Addis, M. E., & Martell, C. R. (2004). *Overcoming depression one step at a time: The new behavioral activation approach to getting your life back.* Oakland, CA: New Harbinger Publications.

This workbook provides a guide to using the strategies of behavioral activation to combat depressive avoidance and re-engage in life. It takes readers through the steps of understanding mood-behavior connections, monitoring behaviors on a daily basis, scheduling behavioral changes to improve mood, and recognizing and modifying avoidance behaviors.

Burns, D. D. (1999). *The feeling good handbook* (rev. ed.). New York: Plume Books.

Based on his highly successful self-help book, *Feeling Good*, Burns offers this handbook complete with exercises and forms that enable readers to monitor thoughts and moods and to practice cognitive restructuring strategies to lead to positive mood shifts.

Greenberger, D., & Padesky, C. A. (1995). *Mind over mood: Change how you feel by changing the way you think.* New York: Guilford Press.

This book presents cognitive therapy for a variety of problems including depression and anxiety. The workbook is full of forms that are useful for monitoring thoughts and behaviors and making plans to change them. Interesting case examples serve as exemplars for the way in which cognitive therapy can improve your life.

Linehan, M. M. (1993). *Skills training manual for treating borderline personality disorder.* New York: Guilford Press.

Linehan's skills training is intended for work in groups of women diagnosed with borderline personality disorder. Regardless of whether such a diagnosis fits you, the workbook is helpful for learning ways to manage difficult emotions and engaging in proactive behaviors that can help you attain a life worth living.

References

Akiskal, H.S. (1995). Mood disorders: Introduction and overview. In H.I. Kaplan & B.J. Sadock (Eds.), *Comprehensive textbook of psychiatry: Vol. 4* (6th ed.). Baltimore: Williams & Wilkins.

American Psychiatric Association (1994, 2000). *Diagnostic and Statistical Manual of Mental Disorders.* Washington, DC: APA.

Andreoli, T. (Ed.). (2001). *CECIL essentials of medicine* (5th ed.). Philadelphia: W. B. Saunders.

Andrews, G., & Harvey, R. (1981). Does psychotherapy benefit neurotic patients? *Archives of General Psychiatry, 38,* 1203.

Angell, M. (2004). The Truth About the Drug Companies: How They Deceive Us and What to Do About It. New York: Random House.

Antonuccio, D.O., Danton, W.G., & DeNelsky, G.Y. (1995). Psychotherapy versus medication for depression: Challenging the conventional wisdom with data. *Professional Psychology: Research and Practice, 26*(6), 574–585.

Antonuccio, D.O. & Naylor, E.V. (2003). Behavioral prescriptions for depression in primary care. In Cummings, N.A., O'Donoqhue, W.J., & Naylor, E.V. (Eds.) (pp. 209–224). *Psychological Approaches to Chronic Disease Management.* Reno, Nevada: Context Press.

Antonuccio, D.O., Thomas, M., & Danton, W.G. (1997). A cost-effectiveness analysis of cognitive behavior therapy and fluoxetine (Prozac) in the treatment of depression. *Behavior Therapy, 28,* 187–210.

Ayllon, T. and Haughton, E. (1962). Control of the behavior of schizophrenic patients by food. *Journal of the Experimental Analysis of Behavior, 5,* 343–352.

Bandura, A. (1963). A social learning interpretation of psychological dysfunctions. In P. London and D. Rosenhan (Eds.), *Foundations of abnormal psychology*. New York: Holt, Rinehart, and Winston.

Bandura, A. (1977). Self-efficacy: Toward a unifying theory of behavioral change. *Psychological Review, 84*, 191–215.

Barlow D. H., Allen, L. B., & Choate, M. L. (2004). Toward a unified treatment of emotional disorders. *Behavior Therapy, 35*(2), 205–230.

Beach, S.R.H., & O'Leary, K. D. (1986). The treatment of depression occurring in the context of marital discord. *Behavior Therapy, 17*, 43–49.

Beck, A. T. (1967). Depression: Causes and treatment. Philadelphia: University of Pennsylvania Press.

Beck, A. T. (1976). *Cognitive therapy and the emotional disorders*. New York: International Universities Press.

Beck, A. T., Resnick, H.L.P., & Lettieri, D.J. (1986). *The prediction of suicide*. Philadelphia: Charles Press.

Beck, A. T., Rush, A.J., Shaw, B.F., & Emery, G. (1979). *Cognitive therapy of depression: A treatment manual*. New York: Guilford Press.

Bellack, A.S., Hersen, M., & Himmelhoch, J. (1981). Social skills training compared with pharmacotherapy and psychotherapy in the treatment of unipolar depression. *American Journal of Psychiatry, 138*, 1562–1566.

Berenson, A. (2005). Despite vow, drug makers still withhold data. *New York Times*, May 31, A1.

Breggin, P. R., & Cohen, D. (2001). *The antidepressant fact book: What your doctor won't tell you about Prozac, Zoloft, Paxil, Celexa and Luvox*. Cambridge, MA: Perseus Books.

Brown, T.A., Campbell, L.A., Lehman, C.L., Grisham, J.R., & Mancill, R.B. (2001). Current and lifetime comorbidity of the DSM-IV anxiety and mood disorders in a large clinical sample. *Journal of Abnormal Psychology, 110*, 49–58.

Cannon, W.B. (1929). Bodily Changes in Pain, Hunger, Fear, and Rage. New York: Appleton.

Chambless, D. L., Baker, M.J., Baucom, D. H., Beutler, L. E., Calhoun, K.S., Crits-Christoph, P., Daiuto, A., DeRubeis, R., Detweiler, J., Haaga, D.A.F., Johnson, S. B., McCurry, S., Mueser, K. T., Pope, K.S., Sanderson, W.C., Shoham, V., Stickle, T., Williams, D.A., & Woody, S.R. (1998). Update on empirically validated therapies, II. *Clinical Psychologist, 51*(1), 3–16.

Chorpita, B. F., & Barlow, D. H. (1998). The development of anxiety: The role of control in the early environment. *Psychological Bulletin, 124*(1), 3–21.

Clarke-Stewart, K.A., Vandell, D. L., McCartney, K., Owen, M. T., & Booth, C. (2000). Effects of parental separation and divorce on very young children. *Journal of Family Psychology, 14*(2), 304–326.

Consumer Reports. (1995). Mental health: Does therapy help? November, 734–739.

Craighead, W.E., Craighead, L.W., & Ilardi, S.S. (1998). Psychosocial treatments for major depressive disorder. In P.E. Nathan and J.M. Gorman (Eds.), *A guide to treatments that work* (pp. 226–248). New York: Oxford University Press.

Craske, M.G., & Barlow, D.H. (2000). *Mastery of your anxiety and panic* (3rd ed.). New York: Graywind Publications.

Depression Guideline Panel (1993). *Depression in primary care: Vol. 2. Treatment of major depression.* Clinical Practice Guideline No. 5, AHCPR Publication No. 93-0551. Rockville, MD: Department of Health and Human Services, Public Health Service, Agency for Health Care Policy and Research.

DeRubeis, R.J., Hollon, S.D., Amsterdam, J.D., Shelton, R.C., Young, P.R., Salomon, R.M., O'Reardon, J.P., Lovett, M.L., Gladis, M.M., Brown, L.L., & Gallop, R. (2005). Cognitive therapy versus medications in the treatment of moderate to severe depression. *Archives of General Psychiatry, 62,* 409–416.

Dimidjian, S., Hollon, S., Dobson, K., Schmaling, K., Kohlenberg, B., McGlinchey, J., Markley, D., Atkins, D., Addis, M., & Dunner, D. (2003). Behavioral activation, cognitive therapy, and antidepressant medications in the treatment of major depression: Design and acute phase outcomes. Paper presented at the 37th Annual Convention of the Association for Advancement of Behavior Therapy, November 21, Boston, MA.

Dollard, J., & Miller, N. (1950). *Personality and psychotherapy.* New York: McGraw-Hill.

Dowling, C. (1993). *You mean I don't have to feel this way: New help for depression, anxiety, and addiction.* New York: Bantam Books.

Duncan, B., Miller, S., & Sparks, J. (2000). Exposing the mythmaking. *Networker,* March/April, 24–53.

Editorial. (2005). Hiding data on drug trials, *New York Times,* June 1, A22.

Elkin, I., Shea, M.T., Watkins, J.T., Imber, S.D., Sotsky, S.M., Collins, J.F., Glass, D.R., Pilkonis, P.A., Leber, W.R., Doherty, J.P., Fiester, S.J., & Parloff, M.B. (1989). NIMH Treatment of Depression Collaboration Research Program: I. General effectiveness of treatments, *Archives of General Psychiatry, 46,* 971–982.

Ellis, A. (1962). *Reason and emotion in psychotherapy.* New York: Lyle Stuart.

Etz Hayim. (2001). *Torah and commentary.* New York: Rabbinical Assembly, Jewish Publication Society.

Ferster, C.B. (1973). A functional analysis of depression. *American Psychologist, 28,* 857–870.

Ferster, C.B., & Perrott, M.C.B. (1968). *Behavior principles.* New York: Appleton-Century-Crofts.

Fisher, S., & Greenberg, R. (Eds.). (1989). *The limits of biological treatments for psychological distress.* Englewood Cliffs, NJ: Lawrence Erlbaum.

Foa, E.B., & Kozack, M.J. (1986). Emotional processing of fear: Exposure to corrective information. *Psychological Bulletin, 99,* 20–35.

Foucault, M. (1965). *Madness and civilization*. New York: Pantheon Books.

Giles, T. R. (1983a). Probable superiority of behavioral interventions—I: Traditional comparative outcome. *Journal of Behavior Therapy and Experimental Psychiatry, 14*, 29–32.

Giles, T. R. (1983b). Probable superiority of behavioral interventions—II: Empirical status of the equivalence of therapies hypothesis. *Journal of Behavior Therapy and Experimental Psychiatry, 14*, 189–196.

Glenmullen, J. (2000). *Prozac backlash: Overcoming the dangers of Prozac, Zoloft, Paxil and other antidepressants with safe, effective alternatives*. New York: Simon & Schuster.

Goldapple, K., Segal, Z., Garson, C., Lau, M., Bieling, P., Kennedy, S., & Mayberg, H. (2004). Modulation of cortical-limbic pathways in major depression: Treatment-specific effects of cognitive behavior therapy. *Archives of General Psychiatry, 61*, 34–41.

Goldfried, M. R., & Trier, C. S. (1974). Effectiveness of relaxation as an active coping skill. *Journal of Abnormal Psychology, 83*, 348–355.

Goozner, M. (2004). Overdosed and oversold. *New York Times*, December 21, A27.

Grant, V. (1956). The development of a theory of heredity. *American Scientist, 44*, 158–179.

Harris, G. (2004a). At FDA, strong drug ties and less monitoring. *New York Times*, December 6, A1.

Harris, G. (2004b). FDA finds drugs linked to suicide. *New York Times*, September 14, A1.

Harris, G. (2004c). FDA panel urges stronger warning on antidepressants. *New York Times*, September 15, A1.

Harris, G. (2004d). FDA's drug safety system will get outside review. *New York Times*, November 6, A11.

Havens, L. (1981). Twentieth century psychiatry: A view from the sea. *American Journal of Psychiatry, 138*, 1279–1287.

Hayes, S. C., Barnes-Holmes, D., & Roche, B. (Eds.). (2001). *Relational frame theory: A post-Skinnerian account of human language and cognition*. New York: Kluwer Academic/Plenum.

Hayes, S. C., Strosahl, K. D., and Wilson, K. G. (1999). *Acceptance and commitment therapy: An experiential approach to behavior change*. New York: Guilford Press.

Hokanson, J. (1983). *Introduction to the therapeutic process*. Reading, MA: Addison-Wesley.

Hollon, M. F. (2005). Direct-to-consumer advertising. A haphazard approach to health promotion. *Journal of the American Medical Association, 293*, 2030–2033.

Hollon, S. D, DeRubeis, R. J., Shelton, R. C., Amsterdam, J. D., Salomon, R. M., O'Reardon, J. P., Lovett, M. L., Young, P. R., Haman, K. L., Freeman, B. B., & Gallop, R. (2005). Prevention of relapse following cognitive therapy versus medications in moderate to severe depression. *Archives of General Psychiatry, 62,* 417–422.

Hollon, S. D., DeRubeis, R. J., Shelton, R. C., & Weiss, B. (2002). The emperor's new drugs: Effect size and moderation effects. *Prevention & Treatment, 5,* Article 28. Retrieved February 5, 2004, from http://journals.apa.org/prevention/volume5/pre0050028c.html.

Hyler, S., Williams, J., and Spitzer, R. (1982). Reliability in the DSM-III field trials. *Archives of General Psychiatry, 39,* 175–178.

Jacobson, E. (1929). *Progressive relaxation.* Chicago: University of Chicago Press.

Jacobson, N. S., & Christensen, A. (1996). Studying the effectiveness of psychotherapy: How well can clinical trials do the job? *American Psychologist, 51*(10), 1031–1039.

Jacobson, N. S., Dobson, K. S., Truax, P. A., Addis, M. E., Koerner, K., Gollan, J. K., Gortner, E., & Prince, S. E. (1996). A component analysis of cognitive-behavioral treatment for depression. *Journal of Consulting and Clinical Psychology, 64*(2), 295–304.

Jacobson, N. S., & Hollon, S. D. (1996). Cognitive-behavior therapy versus pharmacotherapy: Now that the jury's returned its verdict, it's time to present the rest of the evidence. *Journal of Consulting and Clinical Psychology, 64*(1), 74–80.

Jacobson, N. S., Holtzworth-Munroe, A., and Schmaling, K. B. (1989). Marital therapy and spouse involvement in the treatment of depression, agoraphobia, and alcoholism. *Journal of Consulting and Clinical Psychology, 57,* 5–10.

Kadison, R., & DiGeronimo, T. F. (2004). *College of the overwhelmed: The campus mental health crisis and what to do about it.* San Francisco: Jossey-Bass.

Kaufman, M., & Masters, B. (2004). FDA is flexing less muscle. *Washington Post,* November 18, A1.

Kimble, G. (1956). *Principles of general psychology.* New York: Ronald Press.

Kirk, S., & Kutchins, H. (1992). *The selling of the DSM: The rhetoric of science in psychiatry.* New York: Aldine de Gruyter.

Kirsch, I., Moore, T., Scoboria A., & Nicholls, S. S. (2002). The emperor's new drugs: An analysis of antidepressant medication data submitted to the U.S. Food and Drug Administration. *Prevention & Treatment, 5,* Article 23. Retrieved February 5, 2004, from http://journals.apa.org/prevention/volume5/pre0050023a.html.

Klerman, G. (1984). The advantages of DSM-III. *American Journal of Psychiatry, 141,* 539–542.

Klerman, G. (1986). Historical perspectives on contemporary schools of psychopathology. In T. Millon & G. Klerman (Eds.), *Contemporary directions in psychopathology: Toward the DSM-IV.* New York: Guilford Press.

Klerman, G. L., Weissman, M. M., Rounsaville, B. J., & Chevron, E. S. (1984). *Inter-personal psychotherapy of depression.* New York: Basic Books.

Kohlenberg, R. J., & Tsai, M. (1991). *Functional analytic psychotherapy: Creating intense and curative therapeutic relationships.* New York: Plenum Press.

Kravitz, R. L., Epstein, R. M., Feldman, M. D., Franz, C. E., Azari, R., Wilkes, M. S., Hinton, L., & Franks, P. (2005). Influence of patient's requests for direct-to-consumer advertised antidepressants. A randomized controlled trial. *Journal of the American Medical Association, 293,* 1995–2002.

Krupnick, J. L., Sotsky, S. M., Elkin, I., Watkins, J., & Pilkonis, P. A. (1996). The role of the therapeutic alliance in psychotherapy and pharmacotherapy outcome: Findings in the National Institute of Mental Health Treatment of Depression Collaborative Research Program. *Journal of Consulting and Clinical Psychology, 64*(3), 532-539.

Kutchins, H., & Kirk, S. (1997). *The psychiatric bible and the creation of mental disorders.* New York: Free Press.

Lewinsohn, P. M. (1974). A behavioral approach to depression. In R. J. Friedman & M. M. Katz (Eds.), *The psychology of depression: Contemporary theory and research* (pp. 157–178). New York: John Wiley.

Lewinsohn, P. M., Biglan, A., & Zeiss, A. M. (1976). Behavioral treatment of depression. In P. O. Davidson (Ed.), *The behavioral management of anxiety, depression, and pain.* New York: Brunner/Mazell.

Lewinsohn, P., Mischel, W., Chaplin, W., & Barton, R. (1980). Social competence and depression: The role of illusory self-perceptions. *Journal of Abnormal Psychology, 89,* 202–213.

MacPhillamy, D. J., & Lewinsohn, P. M. (1972). The measurement of reinforcing events. *Proceedings of the 80th annual convention of the American Psychological Association, 7,* 399–400.

MacPhillamy, D. J., & Lewinsohn, P. M. (1982). The pleasant events schedule: Studies in reliability, validity, and scale intercorrelation. *Journal of Consulting and Clinical Psychology, 50,* 363–380.

Martell, C. R., Addis, M. E., & Jacobson, N. S. (2001). *Depression in context: Strategies for guided action.* New York: W. W. Norton.

McClintock, M. (1971). Menstrual synchrony and suppression. *Nature, 229,* 244–245.

McClintock, M., & Stern, K. (1998). Regulation of ovulation by human pheromones. *Nature, 392,* 177–179.

Meier, B. (2004). Earlier Merck study indicated risks of Vioxx. *New York Times,* November 18, C1.

Milgram, S. (1963). The behavioral study of obedience. *Journal of Abnormal and Social Psychology, 67,* 371–378.

Miller, N. (1948). Studies of fear as an acquirable drive: I. Fear as motivation and fear-reduction as reinforcement in the learning of new responses. *Journal of Experimental Psychology, 38,* 89–101.

Monroe, S. M., Rohde, P., Seeley, J. R., & Lewinsohn, P. M. (1999). Life events and depression in adolescence: Relationship loss as a prospective risk factor for first onset of major depressive disorder. *Journal of Abnormal Psychology, 108*(4), 606–614.

Moore, T. (1999). It's what's in your head. *The Washingtonian*, October, 45–49.

National College Health Assessment: Reference Group Report. (2002). Baltimore: American College Health Association.

Nelson, B. (1982). Psychiatry's anxious years: Decline in allure; as a career leads to self-examination. *New York Times*, November 2, Section C; Page 1, Column 3; Science Desk.

Newberg, A., Pourdehnad, M., Alavi., d'Aquili, E.G. (2003). Cerebral blood flow during meditative prayer: Preliminary findings and methodological issues. Perceptual and Motor Skills, 97, (2), 625–630.

Newman, T.B. (2004). A black-box warning for antidepressants in children? *New England Journal of Medicine, 351*, 1595–1598.

New Revised Standard Version. (1990). *The Holy Bible*. Nashville, TN: Thomas Nelson Publishers.

Nolen-Hoeksema, S., Morrow, J., & Frederickson, B.L. (1993). Response styles and the duration of episodes of depressed mood. *Journal of Abnormal Psychology, 102*(1), 20–28.

Norden, M.J. (1995). *Beyond Prozac: Brain-toxic lifestyles, natural antidotes & new generation antidepressants.* New York: HarperCollins.

Paul, G.L. (1969). Outcome of systematic desensitization. II. Controlled investigations of individual treatment, technique variations, and current status. In C.M. Franks (Ed.), *Behavior therapy: Appraisal and status*. New York: McGraw-Hill.

Pavlov, I. (1927). *Conditioned reflexes.* Translated by G.V. Anrep. London: Oxford University Press.

Persons, J.B., Thase, M.E., & Crits-Christoph, P., (1996). The role of psychotherapy in the treatment of depression: Review of two practice guidelines. *Archives of General Psychiatry, 53*, 283–290.

Pittu, L. (2002). Mindless psychiatry and dubious ethics. *Counselling Psychology Quarterly, 15*(1), 23–33.

Porter, R. (Ed.) (1996). *Cambridge illustrated history of medicine.* Cambridge, England: Cambridge University Press.

Raimy, V.C. (Ed.). (1950). *Training in clinical psychology.* Englewood Cliffs, NJ: Prentice Hall.

Rehm, L.P. (1977). A self-control model of depression. *Behavior Therapy, 8*, 787–804.

Reinherz, H.A., Giaconia, R.M., Hauf, A.M. Carmola, Wasserman, M.S., & Silverman, A.B. (1999). Major depression in the transition to adulthood: Risks and impairments. *Journal of Abnormal Psychology, 108*(3), 500–510.

Rimm, D., & Masters, J. (1974). *Behavior Therapy.* New York: Academic Press.

Rogers, C. (1951). *Client-centered therapy.* Boston: Houghton Mifflin.

Ross, C., & Pam, A. (1995). *Pseudoscience in biological psychiatry: Blaming the body.* New York: John Wiley.

Safran, J. D., & Segal, Z. V. (1991). *Interpersonal process in cognitive therapy.* New York: Basic Books.

Seligman, M. (1975). *Helplessness: On depression development and death.* San Francisco: W. H. Freeman.

Seligman, M. E. P. (1995). The effectiveness of psychotherapy: The Consumer Reports study. *American Psychologist, 50*(12), 965–974.

Seligman, M., & Maier, S. (1967). Failure to escape traumatic shock. *Journal of Experimental Psychology, 74,* 1–9.

Seminowicz, D. A., Mayberg, H. S., McIntosh, A. R., Goldapple, K., Kennedy, S., Segal, Z., & Rafi-Tari, S. (2004). Limbic-frontal circuitry in major depression: A path modeling metaanalysis. *NeuroImage, 22,* 409–418.

Shea, M. T., Elkin, I., Imber, S. D., Sotsky, S. M., Watkins, J. T., Collins, J. F., Pilkonis, P. A., Beckham, E., Glass, D. R., Dolan, R. T., & Parloff, M. B. (1992). Course of depressive symptoms over follow-up: Findings from the National Institute of Mental Health treatment of depression collaborative research program. *Archives of General Psychiatry, 49,* 782–787.

Shrout, P. E., Link, B. G., Dohrenwend, B. P., Skodol, A. E., Stueve, A., & Mirotznik, J. (1989). Characterizing life events as risk factors for depression: The role of fateful loss events. *Journal of Abnormal Psychology, 98*(4), 460–467.

Singer, C., & Underwood, E. (1962). *A short history of medicine.* New York: Oxford University Press.

Skinner, B. F. (1957). *Verbal behavior.* New York: Appleton-Century-Crofts.

Sloane, R. B., Staples, F. R., Cristol, A. H., Yorkston, N. J., & Whipple, K. (1975). *Psychotherapy versus behavior therapy.* Cambridge, MA: Harvard University Press.

Sommers-Flanagan, J. (1996). Efficacy of antidepressant medication with depressed youth: What psychologists should know. *Professional Psychology: Research and Practice, 27*(2), 145–153.

Spiegel, A. (2005). The dictionary of disorder. *The New Yorker,* January 3, 56–63.

Staats, A., & Staats, C. (1963). *Complex human behavior.* New York: Holt, Rinehart, and Winston.

Stelfox, H., Chua, G., O'Rourke, K., & Detsky, A. (1998). Conflict of interest in the debate over calcium-channel antagonists. *New England Journal of Medicine, 338*(2), 101–106.

Szasz, T. (1974). *The myth of mental illness: Foundations of a theory of personal conduct* (rev. ed.). New York: HarperCollins.

Topol, Eric. (2004). Good riddance to a bad drug. *New York Times,* October 2, A15.

Ullman, L., & Krasner, L. (1969). *A psychological approach to abnormal behavior.* Englewood Cliffs, NJ: Prentice Hall.

U.S. Food and Drug Administration, Center for Drug Evaluation and Research (2004). *Antidepressant use in children, adolescents, and adults.* Retrieved July 5, 2004, from http://www.fda.gov/cder/drug/antidepressants/default.htm.

Valenstein, E.S. (1998). *Blaming the brain: The truth about drugs and mental health.* New York: Free Press.

Vedantam, S. (2004a). Antidepressant use by U.S. adults soars, *Washington Post,* December 3, A15.

Vedantam, S. (2004b). British officials advise less use of antidepressants. *Washington Post,* December 7, A1.

Vedantam, S. (2004c). FDA confirms antidepressants raise children's suicide risk. *Washington Post,* September 14, A1.

Watson, J., & Raynor, R. (1920). Conditioned emotional reactions. *Journal of Experimental Psychology, 3,* 1–14.

Weiss, R. (2004). NIH to set stiff restrictions on outside consulting. *Washington Post,* January 4, A1.

Whitaker, R. (2002). *Mad in America: Bad science, bad medicine, and the enduring mistreatment of the mentally ill.* New York: Perseus Books.

Wolberg, L. (1967). *The technique of psychotherapy.* New York: Grune and Stratton.

Wolfe, S. (2003). Sweetening the pill. *Health Letter,* September 19, 1–10.

Wolfe, S. (2004). Blockbuster arthritis drug rofecoxib (Vioxx) withdrawn from market. *Health Letter,* November 20, 4–5.

Wolpe, J. (1958). *Psychotherapy by reciprocal inhibition.* Stanford, CA: Stanford University Press.

Wolpe, J. (1979). The experimental model and treatment of neurotic depression. *Behavior Research and Therapy, 17,* 555–566.

Zilboorg, G., & Henry, G. (1941). *A history of medical psychology.* New York: W.W. Norton.

Zimbardo, P. (2004). A situationist perspective on the psychology of evil: Understanding how good people are transformed into perpetrators. In A. Miller (Ed.), *The social psychology of good and evil.* New York: Guilford Press.

Index

About the Series Editor and Advisory Board

CHRIS E. STOUT, Psy.D., MBA, is a licensed clinical psychologist and is a clinical full professor at the University of Illinois College of Medicine's Department of Psychiatry. He served as a nongovernmental organization special representative to the United Nations. He was appointed to the World Economic Forum's Global Leaders of Tomorrow, and he has served as an invited faculty at the annual meeting in Davos, Switzerland. He is the founding director of the Center for Global Initiatives. Stout is a fellow of the American Psychological Association, past president of the Illinois Psychological Association, and is a distinguished practitioner in the National Academies of Practice. Stout has published or presented over 300 papers and 30 books and manuals on various topics in psychology. His works have been translated into six languages. He has lectured across the nation and internationally in 19 countries and has visited six continents and almost 70 countries. He was noted as being "one of the most frequently cited psychologists in the scientific literature" in a study by Hartwick College. He is the recipient of the American Psychological Association's International Humanitarian Award.

BRUCE BONECUTTER, Ph.D., is Director of Behavioral Services at the Elgin Community Mental Health Center, the Illinois Department of Human Services state hospital serving adults in greater Chicago. He is also a clinical assistant professor of psychology at the University of

Illinois at Chicago. A clinical psychologist specializing in health, consulting, and forensic psychology, Bonecutter is a longtime member of the American Psychological Association Task Force on Children and the Family. He is a member of the Association for the Treatment of Sexual Abusers, International, the Alliance for the Mentally Ill, and the Mental Health Association of Illinois.

JOSEPH FLAHERTY, M.D., is chief of psychiatry at the University of Illinois Hospital, a professor of psychiatry at the University of Illinois College of Medicine, and a professor of community health science at the UIC College of Public Health. He is a founding member of the Society for the Study of Culture and Psychiatry. Flaherty has been a consultant to the World Health Organization, the National Institute of Mental Health, and the Falk Institute in Jerusalem. He's been director of undergraduate education and graduate education in the Department of Psychiatry at the University of Illinois. Flaherty has also been staff psychiatrist and chief of psychiatry at Veterans Administration West Side Hospital in Chicago.

MICHAEL HOROWITZ, Ph.D., is president and professor of clinical psychology at the Chicago School of Professional Psychology, one of the nation's leading not-for-profit graduate schools of psychology. Earlier, he served as dean and professor of the Arizona School of Professional Psychology. A clinical psychologist practicing independently since 1987, his work has focused on psychoanalysis, intensive individual therapy, and couples therapy. He has provided disaster mental health services to the American Red Cross. Horowitz's special interests include the study of fatherhood.

SHELDON I. MILLER, M.D., is a professor of psychiatry at Northwestern University, and director of the Stone Institute of Psychiatry at Northwestern Memorial Hospital. He is also director of the American Board of Psychiatry and Neurology, director of the American Board of Emergency Medicine, and director of the Accreditation Council for Graduate Medical Education. Miller is also an examiner for the American Board of Psychiatry and Neurology. He is founding editor of the *American Journal of Addictions* and founding chairman of the American Psychiatric Association's Committee on Alcoholism. Miller has also been a lieutenant commander in the military, serving as psychiatric consultant to the Navajo Area Indian Health Service at Window Rock, Arizona. He is a member and past president of the

Executive Committee for the American Academy of Psychiatrists in Alcoholism and Addictions.

DENNIS P. MORRISON, Ph.D., is chief executive officer at the Center for Behavioral Health in Indiana, the first behavioral health company ever to win the Joint Commission on Accreditation of Health Care Organizations Codman Award for excellence in the use of outcomes management to achieve health care quality improvement. He is president of the board of directors for the Community Healthcare Foundation in Bloomington and has been a member of the board of directors for the American College of Sports Psychology. He has served as a consultant to agencies including the Ohio Department of Mental Health, Tennessee Association of Mental Health Organizations, Oklahoma Psychological Association, North Carolina Council of Community Mental Health Centers, and the National Center for Health Promotion in Michigan.

WILLIAM H. REID, M.D., is a clinical and forensic psychiatrist and a consultant to attorneys and courts throughout the United States. He is a clinical professor of psychiatry at the University of Texas Health Science Center. Reid is also an adjunct professor of psychiatry at Texas A&M College of Medicine and Texas Tech University School of Medicine, as well as a clinical faculty member at the Austin Psychiatry Residency Program. He is chairman of the Scientific Advisory Board and medical advisor to the Texas Depressive & Manic Depressive Association as well as an examiner for the American Board of Psychiatry and Neurology. He has served as president of the American Academy of Psychiatry and the Law, chairman of the research section for an International Conference on the Psychiatric Aspects of Terrorism, and medical director for the Texas Department of Mental Health and Mental Retardation. Reid earned an Exemplary Psychiatrist Award from the National Alliance for the Mentally Ill. He has been cited on the Best Doctors in America listing since 1998.

About the Authors

ALLAN M. LEVENTHAL, PhD, is Professor Emeritus of Psychology at American University, where he also served as Director of the Counseling Center. He is a Diplomate in Clinical Psychology with the American Board of Professional Psychology, a Fellow of the American Psychological Association, and past president of the Maryland Psychological Association, as well as past chairman of the Maryland State Board of Examiners of Psychologists. Until his retirement last year he was engaged in the out-patient practice of psychology for more than twenty-five years. He is the recipient of an Outstanding Psychologist Award from the Maryland Psychological Association.

MARSHA LINEHAN, Ph.D. is a Professor of Psychology, Adjunct Professor of Psychiatry and Behavioral Sciences at the University of Washington and Director of the Behavioral Research and Therapy Clinics. She has written three books, including two treatment manuals: *Cognitive-Behavioral Treatment for Borderline Personality Disorder* and *Skills Training Manual for Treating Borderline Personality Disorder.* She serves on a number of editorial boards and has published extensively in scientific journals.

CHRISTOPER R. MARTELL, PhD, is Clinical Associate Professor at the University of Washington, and a psychologist in private practice in Seattle. He is a Diplomate in Clinical Psychology and Behavioral

Psychology with the American Board of Professional Psychology, and a Fellow of the American Psychological Association. He is past president of the Washington State Psychological Association, a founding fellow of the Academy of Cognitive Therapy, and recipient of the 2004 Washington State Psychological Association's Distinguished Psychologist award.